SINGING LIGHT

SINGING LIGHT

Becoming Me

SONDRA MARKIM

Full Court Press
Englewood Cliffs, New Jersey

First Edition

Copyright © 2017 by Sondra Markim

All rights reserved. No part of this book may be reproduced or transmitted in any form or by any means electronic or mechanical, including by photocopying, by recording, or by any information storage and retrieval system, without the express permission of the author,
except where permitted by law.

Published in the United States of America
by Full Court Press, 601 Palisade Avenue,
Englewood Cliffs, NJ 07632
fullcourtpressnj.com

ISBN 978-1-946989-08-6
Library of Congress Catalog No. 2017962169

*Editing and book design by Barry Sheinkopf
for Bookshapers (bookshapers.com)*

"In my craft or sullen art
Exercised in the still night
When only the moon rages
And the lovers lie abed
With all their griefs in their arms
I labour by singing light
Not for ambition or bread
Or the strut and trade of charms
On the ivory stages
But for the common wages
Of their most secret heart."

—*Dylan Thomas*

I write these words by *my* singing light—
to cast a shadow on this earth,
that I was here, I mattered.

Prologue

IN REVISITING A LIFE BRIMMING with sensory images, I wonder whether I have the chops to adequately do it justice here. I also wonder whom it is I'm writing to. Myself? Like a diary or therapy, working out emotions, processing, internalizing to make sense of it? Or perhaps more like leaving my pyramid—Hey, World, I was here! Or to my children, settings things straight and expressing things I should have said before but haven't?

Assessing my past through the lens of the Me of today as I filter through the dull parts requires me to confront and navigate events that not only had an impact but that, being dredged up, gave oxygen to many painful, egregious feelings. For the sake of expediency, I sometimes sacrifice nuance, too. Merely conjuring up all the *Sturm und Drang* could seem either derivative or self-promoting—for example, listing all the men in my life, or some of the accolades I've received (fist bumps to my needy ego).

But how can a memoir, by definition, *not* be self-centered?

Not to cop out while I'm shamefully doing just that, I therefore plead for poetic leeway, because I am tethered to the limits of human fallibility with no precise algorithms to guide me. I can only consult my own experience and allow my story to unspool. As I delve, I dive in.

I have no intention or hidden agenda here beyond telling my story through a prism of memories that drive it and compel me to point out that the tale is an explanation, not an excuse (my grandchildren may want to skip some chapters), and at best perhaps provide a few useful lessons about what I've learned during my time on Earth.

I'm also writing a testament to love, for this is a love story—partly for the child in me who didn't get enough of it, but also to the adult survivor healed by the love of my husband.

Thus I dedicate this book to my healer, the memory of Al Markim.

Unpacking My Baggage

I WAS UNABLE TO FALL ASLEEP, even with my devices for boring myself there: the multiplication tables, or reciting the States alphabetically. So I tried recalling my earliest memory.

Likely informed by memory-laden photos or passed-on lore, I fixed on the time I was three, living with my divorced mother and seven-year-old sister at the boarding house run by my grandparents. I've since learned it was actually a flophouse! This sparked vivid memories of helping Grandma change sheets under her stern, watchful eyes...being terrified of tiny bugs on the walls near the beds and the unpleasant smell of my grandfather's old leather shoes, their phonograph you wound up with its two recordings: "Yes, We Have No Bananas" and "Amapola" (which I thought was "I'm a Polack," bewildered why my singing those words elicited snickers).

I've heard stories that my grandmother, upon leaving Europe with her family to move to Chicago, learned to drive a car but preferred driving it on sidewalks because the streets were too crowded. . .and that Grandma's cheerful husband, "Tati" (who was nothing like her), with his round cherubic face and crinkly smiling eyes, had walked the Carpathian Mountains with his son, my uncle Joe, and single-handedly killed a bear. But aside from anecdotal lore, first- hand memories in the form of odd fragments flood my mind: at breakfast, having to drink hot water and orange juice from small glasses (which had once contained religious candles), all the more odd since my grandparents, who thought milk was bad for you, had owned a small goat milk farm in their native Hungary.

Things I liked were playing beauty parlor and combing the few hairs on my grandfather's bald head. . .playing dominoes with my grandmother when she had time and while Mother was away at her job as a telephone operator at Mount Sinai hospital. where I was born. . .and playing with their two big German police dogs who, on occasion, babysat for me and my sister, seven-year old Eileen—four years older than I. Even boredom sticks out vividly: having nothing to do but take a stick and poke at ants on the sidewalk. Tearing up leaves, putting them in an old bowl and pretending I was cooking them. Picking my nose, making a little ball with the snot and flinging it or sticking it down on the wall next to my bed where mother couldn't see. (Who had tissues in those days?)

Two exciting ones: my Uncle Mike doing magic tricks pulling a penny out of my ear!. . .my mother dressing me in something like a costume for Halloween (a rare happy time with her). . .being bribed to say the *fier kashas* (the Four Questions) at the *seder*, spawning my first delicious taste of lavished attention. Though painfully bashful and uncomfortable with it, I doubtless was seduced by that attention. I eventually succumbed to their prodding to say the *kashas* with the promise of a new dress and, as I write this, on my bedroom wall hangs a large framed photo of a three-year-old green-eyed girl in a red dress, a red bow atop blonde curls, wearing the glimmer of a Mona Lisa smile.

Fully engaged in the memory game and therefore totally awake, another flashback unfurled: staying overnight at an aunt's and, years later, when I happened to describe the peculiar and particular circumstances, her house and so on, being told that I had to have been only two, since that was the only time I was ever there. But what sticks out most about that time was being upset when my mother was leaving and I heard someone tell her, "We'll pick you up at four, Helen." Why? I wondered. Was she going to fall down?

So I was two; my earliest memory. But then I had another question for me. When was the first time I was conscious of being me.

Can you remember when you knew you were you? I have examined this thought before and remember quite clearly being four years old and living at the Austin Arms hotel with my mother, sister, and new stepfather. There was very little to do there, I was not allowed to go beyond the front steps, my big sister wanted nothing to do with me, and I had no friends but a next-door neighbor who was a kind woman, seemed to want to befriend me, and would often stop to talk with me. She told my mother that, if ever my mother wanted to let me go, she'd adopt me.

One day she gave me a little tin mirror that had a picture of a heart on the other side of it. She told me to keep the mirror and, any time I felt lonely or sad, to look into it and see how pretty and good I was. I kept it as though it were godly. I know I was aware of me looking at me and thinking the most important thing in the world was for me to be a good girl, which I would tell myself in the mirror repeatedly. That is when I knew I was me.

A lifetime ago.

Fast forward eighty years. It's the next day, and I'm hungry, which often happens when I'm tired and don't get enough sleep. But the juices of my history are flowing, and I think maybe I'll let them.

Art

THUS, I'M IN MY KITCHEN, making a PBJ and banana sandwich and flashing back to when I was nine, a happy time in my otherwise not so happy childhood. Mother made those peanut butter sandwiches, my favorite, and packed them up, along with her four daughters, all a-titter, sparkly-eyed, and full of liquid laughter, as we boarded the Roosevelt Road streetcar, where we sat impatiently until the end of the line where glorious Lake Michigan awaited just a short trek to the beach. Merely trading the blisteringly stifling air of our pitiful West Side neighborhood redolent of garbage and, at times, worse—the rotting meat from the nearby stockyards—for the fresh, breezy beach air was heaven by itself, but mother giving us her rare undivided time was double heaven!

My sisters Eileen and Dorothy would splash around with me in the cool, delicious water, deliriously overjoyed. We'd never want to leave, and if I had to tinkle, did it there, naughtily amused by the warm secret streaming between my legs. Sometimes we'd float on a rubber inner tube, hating to share or for the day to end. We'd also potchky around on the sand (I had a knack for sculpting full-length people out of sand that elicited admiration from people, which of course I lapped up) until lunch time, when we'd run, dripping wet and breathless, to the grassy part of the beach where Mother, smelling like citronella, would be sitting on a blanket along with baby Vivien, who might be napping or busying herself with some toy, a sun hat on and her body slathered with white creamy sun goo. We'd gobble up our wilted, sticky (and sandy), but delicious PBJ sandwiches, eager to get back to the water but forced to wait out the allotted Digesting Time, an eternity, so maybe we'd do something like play One Potato Two Potato or peel the dead, dry skin off our sunburnt bodies.

It was there on the blanket that I vaguely recall a man, lying nearby, staring at us.

Being nine, barely dry beyond my years, and into my own world, I probably would never have paid him any mind except perhaps to fleetingly notice his pale green eyes over a sad, half-moon smile, but what cements that moment and imprints it indelibly was my mother doing an unprecedented thing by suggesting I offer him some grapes. Offer grapes to a *stranger*? The biggest no-no in our family was to speak to strangers, because we lived in one of Chicago's most dangerous slums, and we were there because it was where the Robinson Dairy was, and my stepfather was Jack Robinson.

No doubt I was dumbstruck, but, obedient child that I was in those days, I reluctantly crept over and held out my fist of grapes.

SINGING LIGHT

My next recollection of him happened not long afterward, when another shattering event took place. Mother singled me out to go shopping with her, which in itself wasn't unusual, but what was, aside from her wearing lipstick and rouge, was her prodding me to walk way past the grocery store until she pointed to a big, beautiful parked car and told me to get in!

Inside was the grape man. How she explained him to me is lost on me now, but I would learn his name was Art, an Old Friend.

I sat enthralled in the back of his big, sumptuously comfortable car, marveling at it, my hands sliding across the smooth leather seats—so different from the yucky mohair ones in my stepfather's old Chevy that reeked of cigar smoke—completely transported by the enchanting and unreal turn of events. Mother's voice had changed, was different somehow, soft and melodic like those of Ladies in Movies, not her usual strident one. Stunned, I was thrilled, *not knowing what would happen next*—something that I couldn't know then would later become addictive. It was as though I had folded into a new me, confused but ready for anything.

They sat in the front, laughing and talking for what seemed a long time, rather ignoring me, which I didn't mind, grateful for something *new*. From my low point of view, Art's looks were okay enough. Tall and stocky, with light brown hair and a large forehead, he was no Alan Ladd, but he wasn't ugly. He was obviously taken with Mother all girlish and googly-eyed as she flipped her dark wavy hair away from her face, which people said was beautiful, though I didn't think so. She did have two things I wanted: her dimples (I'd stick a pencil to my cheeks to make them), and her large breasts (I'd sometimes stick rolled-up socks in my undershirt to form them). But I didn't know why everyone said she was a beauty. I usually saw her in an old chintz house dress, her dark hair wrapped in a bandanna, often with some beads of sweat on her tight-faced upper lip or armpits, or between her breasts as she did her endless chores.

Art drove us far off into a strange neighborhood and stopped at the dreamiest restaurant I'd ever seen. It had thick carpeting, soft music, friendly waiters, and big plush cotton napkins on a cloth-covered table capped by a small vase of real flowers. I felt transported into a Hollywood movie. The rare times my family went out to eat were to the little dingy Chinese restaurant in our neighborhood with puke-yellow lights so dim you hardly noticed the grease-smudged menus or the flies stuck to a hanging cylinder. Sweaty-smelling waiters would be impatient with me because, a "difficult eater," I didn't like food in general or theirs in particular. (Often I'd sit at the dinner table for a half hour or so before I swallowed the spoonful of my mother's yucky chicken soup.) I'd eventually settle on *egg foo yung* because it was sort of like an omelet and I'd pick at it throughout the meal. I knew my family liked it because it was cheap.

Art ordered me an enormous club sandwich with a chocolate malted, not seeming to care how expensive it was. It was the most delicious thing ever in my whole mouth! Remarkably, I'd never seen my mother so cheery or thought she smelled so good. She seemed softer and girlish, often joining Art laughing at my cute little jokes, another first for her. That must have encouraged me to keep trying to be what I thought was adorable until her stern eyes gave me a familiar look and I gave it up. What I didn't give up was thinking that I was in a dream and finally the princess I'd been meant to be. My only problem was my bashfulness, causing me to burn with embarrassment at how intimately friendly they were with each other. Innately I sensed something was off, but I made myself not care.

Art left us quite a distance from familiar territory, and as we walked toward the grocery store my mother told me the most thrilling thing she ever had: Art was my fairy godfather! She made me swear to secrecy on my life to keep it between us, which I was only too happy to do since it was our own secret that I could mentally lord over my excluded sisters, because I was *nyeh-nyeh* special! Indeed, I fell right into the game of conspiracy like second nature. Playacting, which was really lying, was super fun, and it was exciting being a spy, all helpful and important. So if Daddy, my stepfather, were home, I'd take the phone pretending it was for me. I'd pull down the front window shade as some other sort of signal to Art. It was I whom mother pretended to be going with somewhere and then get into Art's beautiful car, which, during the freezing Chicago winters, was gloriously, scrumptiously warm and blissful inside. Cinderella not only had a fairy godfather but also a carriage!

Initially I didn't question any of these arrangements because, at that age, I lived immersed in fairy-tales. I'd read every one I could find at the library or school. Religiously, I'd listen to *Let's Pretend* on the radio Saturday mornings. I saw *Fantasia* in the movies over and over. I created fantasies and my own fairytales, my imagination easily allowing Cinderella to escape from her toxic home of fights or boredom, transcending to a custom-made one. As I lay abed, two tissues or two bobby pins could be a girl and a boy, my bent knees forming the backdrop, mountains and caves, and my imagination unfolding a tale. On paper I endlessly wrote made-up songs, poems, drew pictures, and created a myriad of entertainments that came easily to me, diversions that served me well. The lower-grade teachers in school must have been told I had some sort of talent, since they'd periodically seek permission from my teacher for me to go down to their classes and, as a special treat for their kids, tell my stories. There I'd stand in front of the class, confidently reciting and improvising as I went along—surely, preparation that would one day galvanize me toward the assurance I'd need for my eventual acting career.

To my mind then it was totally reasonable that Art was my fairy godfather.

It wasn't so long after the Depression, but "Daddy," being the owner of Robinson Dairy, was not poor. He was, however, penurious to a fault. Mother had to account in a special ledger for every single penny she spent. Literally. I had no toys except for a doll, Monopoly, and roller skates. Of course there was no television then, and we were not allowed to play with the "low-class" non-Jewish neighborhood children, though I did anyway, my first male friend a "colored boy" and my best girl friend Irish. Long, boring summer days offered little fun, so that busting tar bubbles off the asphalt streets was one activity, and in winter, sticking pennies on the Jack-Frosted window, making patterns, another. My sisters and I, confined to playing in the gated yard where they parked the dairy trucks, would slip and slide on drips and drabs of curdled spilled milk, constantly bruising or cutting ourselves on broken milk bottle glass, unmindful of it.

For the next six years or so I never questioned the fact of Art. I also never stopped being shy with him though I felt the trade-off of feeling special was worth any discomfort. My joy, however, was accompanied by unintended complications. When we were home, Mother reverted to her usual short-tempered, harsh ways. I remember her calling me "Honey" once. Once. The rest of the time, she was usually yelling at or berating me or, when I got older, beating me up. She actually broke my finger when I was just a few months more than eighteen years old and married. (I had it fixed at Stanford University Hospital, where I lived—as the then-wife of a student—ignorant of the arthritic pain it would cause me down the line in my eighties.)

Clearly, the relationship with Art didn't transform her, and in hindsight I imagine the very fact we were in cahoots, necessitating her having to reveal herself, as it were, only served to heighten her resentment of me. Nor was it a truly fairy godfather situation for me either, in the sense that he couldn't lavish me with gifts or they would be noticed. Only once, around my birthday, my whole family was walking in the park and mother pointed down to the grass where she "saw something" nobody else did and told me to go see what it was. My palm surreptitiously opened, and lo, there was a gold ring in the grass with, of all things, an *S* on it, my very own initial! Another time I got a pretty necklace with a Jewish star surrounded by tiny jewels. What the pretense was for that, I forget.

It wouldn't be until I was fifteen that I mustered the courage to ask Art if he was my real father. He hemmed and hawed, not answering, and cut off the discussion. It seemed to me he only wanted to take us to lunch or sit in the parked car somewhere, the three of us singing, his pinky ring tapping to the beat on the steering wheel. With misty eyes, he'd croon to mother, "If You Are but a Dream," "I'm Always Chasing Rainbows," or "Ah, Sweet Mystery of Life." Occasionally they'd kiss long, sloppy kisses, which I dreaded, so I'd busy myself either picking on a cuticle or staring at something out the back seat window, probably sucking on a strand of hair, which I often did when I was hungry or uncomfortable.

Growing up acutely aware of their unfulfilled love put a real hurt on me, as my heart bled for them. I prayed every night they'd find a way to be together. When I asked why they didn't get married, Mother explained she'd lose her two younger daughters to Jack because Dorothy and Vivien were true Robinsons. Although my sisters could be a pain, I too feared losing them. So from age nine until I was a grown woman with a child of my own, I suffered with them their lifetime of deprivation and unrequited love. It was from that tender age I would grow to know two things: Life was dramatically sad, and grown-ups didn't always have to follow the rules, including marital fidelity.

Many years later, after a lifetime of that, they were finally free to marry but didn't. They had lost something. I never understood it, but it was gone.

Ah, sweet misery of life.

Origins (A Score Card)

FOR ME, IN THE BEGINNING were Art and Helen. Somebody ate the proverbial apple, I guess, and the end result was they begat.

Dialing it back, before I go on, I should explain that Helen's first husband was a tough named Eddie Smith. Family lore had it he was in the Jewish Mafia and had killed a brother or someone. I know very little about that, except that they'd had a child they named Eileen and that he'd become abusive to Helen, and one day they'd had a fight ending with Eddie hitting Helen, so she'd grabbed Eileen and rushed over to her best friend Leota's house. Leota happened to be having a party for a few of her single girl friends, to introduce them to a handsome bachelor she knew in the hope of a connection for one of them. Years later, Art told me, "When your mother, the most beautiful woman I'd ever seen, walked in, that was it. I only had eyes for her."

Obviously it was mutual, because they hooked up long enough

for her to, as people put it then, "get caught." Abortions were out of the question in 1933, and coming from very religious homes it would have been a disgrace to have a baby out of wedlock. The only recourse was for Helen to return to Eddie's bed and pretend the baby was his. Enter Sondra, stage wrong.

So I'm a bastard or, as I prefer to think, a "love child."

Mother stuck it out with Eddie long enough to have me and lasted about three years more, until she was unable to take it any longer. Under Jewish law, to get a divorce one needs to obtain a document called a *get*. In order to get Eddie to comply, he insisted that she give up all financial support. This was the Depression. But she caved. Penniless, she went to live with her parents in their boarding house, along with her toddler Eileen and me.

Helen was finally free, but Art was nowhere to be found, having left Chicago broken-hearted. Utterly dejected and thinking life couldn't get any worse, Helen went to a Jewish People's Institute (JPI) dance where she met Jack Robinson, who later proposed to her. Hoping for the best—and pressured not to be a burden to her financially strapped parents, since he was willing to take care of her and her two children—she accepted his proposal. So she went from Eddie the frying pan into Jack the fire.

Talk about timing! Events turned exponentially worse. Art eventually returned to Chicago and, upon hearing Helen had gotten divorced but remarried, was totally discouraged. A young, virile man three years younger than Helen, he met a woman, married, and had two daughters of his own.

Several years went by (I'm aware of how melodramatic this sounds—I almost expect to hear the swell of organ music!).

In any event, poor Mother never had any luck in the love department. It didn't take long for her to realize that the mojo with Jack Robinson had gone bad, too. Perhaps she had never gotten over Art and never truly cared for Jack, or perhaps, having gotten pregnant with me, which forced her to live with Eddie and screw up her life is why she was always so angry with me. Anyway, she got pregnant again and this time decided to stick it out for the long haul.

Where, when, and how they resumed their relationship, I've no clue, except that, as I've said, Art popped back into her life when I was nine, this time with *both* of them married to others.

I could continue about how miserable they both were, and the consequences affecting our lives, but I'll spare you. You're welcome.

Daddy

MY FAILED MARRIAGES were a close second in the triumvirate of my Worst Experiences. But the first and most difficult one to describe is Jack Robinson.

In my earliest memory of him, I'm four, in pajamas with footies. It is evening, and he's been living with us, my mother, Eileen, and me, for a short while. He's eating dinner in the kitchenette of our cute apartment in Oak Park, and I crawl up on a chair to sit near him. I meekly ask if I can call him "Daddy." Slurping red borscht, he truculently consents.

Rewinding to that age, little surfaces. I know I slept in the same bed with Eileen, a comfort because I had nightmares over my first scary movie, *Dr. Kildare's Cabinet*. I also know we were in Oak Park long enough for me to go to kindergarten, which accepted four-year-olds. I made a paper fan there and worked hard on it, but before they passed them out to us, I had to go to the hospital with appendicitis. During that time we moved to the West

Side, where the dairy was, and I never got my fan. It wasn't fair. Seventy-eight years ago, I still remember it like yesterday. That fan was my "Rosebud."

But I see him, my new stepfather, clearly. He reminded me of a gorilla, short and squat with long, hairy arms. He had a Russian-looking face that I later thought resembled the actor Edward G. Robinson's, complete with bushy black eyebrows and a fat cigar constantly lodged between his thick lips.

I don't remember much else about that time except we moved from the Oak Park apartment to the West Side with baby Dorothy in tow. And the honeymoon was clearly over. Jack Robinson was a tyrant who got a cook, cleaning woman, nurse, seamstress, vagina, and uterus in their bargain, and we got room and board. Between my parents' endless bickering and screaming, their voices at the volume of a lion's roar, I developed a sort of immunity. A thrumming of volcanic hostility in the air permeated with the constant cacophony of my sisters and me (all squinchy-eyed, thrust-chinned, and clench-fisted), accompanied by our atonal music: whining, screeching, growling, crying, accompanied by the lyrics "I did not! You did, too! I hate you! I'm telling!" On the rare tranquil evenings when there was calm and everyone was sitting in the living room listening to the radio to fun shows like *Lux Radio Theatre* or sometimes dull junk like Gabriel Heater or war news, mother might be darning socks or folding diapers because we now had baby Vivien (making four daughters all four years apart). Daddy would be sitting at a table, playing solitaire, I'd be lying on the carpet—I see me in my pink chenille robe, not very neatly cutting out paper dolls or coloring in a coloring book, doubtless out of the lines. If Eileen was in a good mood, she'd play a game with me like Monopoly, and, with bratty Dorothy and crybaby Vivien too young to stay up, I'd have a sense of peace. But that was pitifully rare.

So from age nine, when I first met Art and became their beard, I tried finding some equilibrium as a "normal" child.

But then at age ten, my life would be thrust upon an inexorable path one evening, wresting innocence and trust, leaving in its wake insecurity and bottomless need—damaged goods, the Me I was no longer.

In bed about to go to sleep, I was surprised yet pleased when Daddy came unprecedentedly into my room to say goodnight. I was delighted and grateful for any parental tenderness or affection.

What is indelibly fixed in my head was his bending over my bed, stroking my forehead, and asking if I had been a good girl that day. Any joy I might have had at this unusual gesture of affection segued into stark confusion when he began stroking my chest beneath my pajamas. Suddenly I felt awash with a tingly, new, yet not unpleasant sensation as his gentle fingers massaged lower onto my belly. I can only describe the moment as a combination of confusion, fear, and excitement. He whispered in my ear, "Do you like that?" Perhaps I sensed he wanted me to appreciate his efforts, and I sort of did, so I nodded.

When his gentle stroking crept lower still to a part of my body I had no name for, a new feeling overwhelmed and took my breath away. I believe that, at that transformative moment, a familiar door closed and an alien one opened, bleeding a sort of virus that invaded and conflated innocence into an ungodly enlightenment. I don't know how else to explain the effect that metastasizing event had on my ten-year-old psyche, but at its least damaging it established a hyper-vigilance—about falling asleep with nightmares of a monster chasing me—for years to come. At its worst, it destroyed dignity and trust, imprisoning me in its toxic orbit. Regardless of how melodramatic it may sound, I believe those fingers burnished and festered and altered the contours of my life!

Compounding this, he extracted a promise not to tell anyone because if I did, "someone could get killed." Even worse, and the thing that plagues me yet, is when he asked me, "Do you want me to stop?" I couldn't tell him not to.

So not only was I the consequence of a secret liaison with my mother unfaithful to her husband, but I'd become trapped in the same sick mire with him.

Although he never did anything more than use his hands—those fingers—to grope and fondle, which occurred on and off for several years, he did his damage, and I lived through those years abhorring those moments, balancing both my parents' secrets juxtaposed against the struggle to maintain a semblance of normalcy. I wonder to this day how I did as well as I did in school. Somehow I internalized and compartmentalized that part of my life as a mere oddity to keep forgetting about, constantly brushing it away.

One might ask why my mother never questioned Daddy's attention to me, entering my bedroom so frequently: None so blind as those who will not see?

It has been said that victims of incest are second only to victims of the Holocaust in the damage they bear. The enormity of its effect on me cannot be measured.

A remark of James Agee wrote resonated in me for years:

"We are like mirrors, locked face to face in an endless corridor of despair."

Chameleon

BUT SMARTY PANTS THAT I WAS, in second grade they skipped me. Stanford-Binet IQ tests indicated 130, but the turmoil of my home life left its mark. I couldn't grasp math to save my life. I ascribe this to two contributing factors. One, they skipped me; and, two, my parents took me out of school at the start of the basic rudimentaries of arithmetic, and we traveled for a month across the country with nothing but a little lesson book, which eluded me (and my parents, telling me to learn by myself, didn't help). When I got back to school, the kids were so ahead, leaving me feeling so defeated that I stopped trying. (Even today I ask waiters how much tip I should leave if I don't have Suri handy.)

Right-brained, however, I did excel in anything artistic, earning all sorts of awards. (I put my toe in that door of success later in life with an art show in New York, selling several pieces, my specialty being full-length *papier-mâché* people. And the Betty Ford

Center in California accepted one of my pieces. If the definition of "professional" is that you are paid for your work, I've been a professional singer, actress, dancer, model, songwriter, writer, and artist—small "a"—all evidence of the right brain at work.)

I can attribute my lack of confidence over these achievements to my early history, but one would think that, after four and a half years of therapy and countless ones with a loving husband, I'd have more self-assurance. But even today my astute daughter can tell whom I'm talking to on the phone merely by my tone and inflection: lack of a well-integrated ego, no doubt. For example, if I'm talking to a Southerner, my Southern persona materializes, and so on. It's as if I search to find where I fit.

I've frequently been told I never look the same two days in a row, through a change in my hairdo or whatever. Photos of me verify that, because I look very differently from one to the next. I am much better at not being a chameleon now, but when I was young it was another story. I'd simply take on the vestiges of whomever I was with.

So I went from Prissy Sondra, the demure and polite four-or-so-year-old, to the feisty daredevil tomboy of eight or so, very Street: jitter-bugging and Double-Dutch jump roping with the black kids of the Nabe, and then, *ba-da-bing, yo!* I went to the mostly Italian middle school, trying to be cool and bad-ass with the duck-ass haired Nunzio Tisci, Jack Accardi, and Anthony Carbone, and ultra-cool girls like Geraldine Molinari and Betty Trotti (with me insisting I was part Italian because my uncle Jim, my stepfather's brother, was married to an Italian). Then being uprooted, up-heaved, and transferred, at age eleven, to a Hebrew parochial school, where I was, *oy vey*, way over my head in a land of weird orthodox yarmulke-wearing Jews who only spoke Hebrew!

And that was, like, Big Time Serious change: I had to learn hieroglyphic Hebrew! Even my name was no longer Sondra, but my Hebrew one, Tsvia. I had to juggle regular school from nine to three and Hebrew studies from three to five. Although it was mind-bogglingly arduous, in time the burden grew lighter because I fell in love with my fellow Zionist friends and, with a new fervor, joined them in their Causes for Israel. So now color me fiercely proud, militant, teen-aged Jewess Sondra (Tsvia), who joined organizations such as the Shomar Hadati and Poel Mizrachi amid weekend youth group meetings with vigorous discussions of all aspects of Jewish life and religion. For a short time my parents coughed up the dough so I could go to a Zionist communal camp for two weeks where, at the tender age of fifteen, I became even more engaged with the all pervasive Zionist, Jewish movement, as well as falling in love with a boy named Dov, the first to hold my hand and kiss me.

One moment in particular I still remember with great fondness: It was an exquisite evening at Camp Moshovat in Ashland, Wisconsin. Clean, crisp air resplendent with the scent of nearby pines offered a rare and invigorating treat. The two weeks there would be my only time at a camp and also away from my miserable home. That night, the kids had built an enormous wooden Mogen David (star of Israel), which they set afire, and we sat around it under the starlit sky with the warm firelight reflecting joy on our faces as we sang beautiful Hebrew songs and talked endlessly about the meaning of things like God and Goodness, feeling certain nobody but us ever had. Later we joined hands and danced the *Hora* around the fire until it and we were exhausted. I had never felt more like I belonged.

As I said, only Hebrew was spoken. How I got by with the mumbo-jumbo of that language is beyond me. I smile remembering how once, in the lunch tent, someone asked me to pass an item, in Hebrew of course: "Tsvia, *ten lee, b'vakasha*. . .blah blah . . .peanut butter"!

Since I lived too far from my new religious world to walk to the Zionist meetings, and public transportation on the Sabbath was forbidden, I often stayed with my local friends on weekends. There were times I couldn't finagle an invitation but, desperately wanting to be with them, feigning I was as Orthodox as they, I pretended I had a relative who lived nearby and at whose house I would be staying, enabling me to simply walk over to the meeting place. To execute my plot, I took our nearby streetcar and rode it two-thirds of the way sitting up like a normal person, telling myself I was a good Jew like the rest of my friends, with dispensation from Above. But Myself wasn't buying it. When I got close to their neighborhood, I slunk very low on the seat till the stop before the designated one and then shrunk as I snuck off the streetcar, praying I was invisible. Some of my pals were so Orthodox that if a boy, say, worked in the lunchroom as a cashier, he would toss the change either on the counter or drop it in your palm, careful not to touch your skin if you were a girl because you could be *tomay*, which meant dirty (that is, having your period). For quite a while I got away with living my little white lie of being like one of them, but then one fateful day I slipped, forgetting an important no-no—*not* turning on a light on the Sabbath! At the Poel Mizrachi meeting room, the day had grown dark. Without thinking, I switched on the light to an instant chorus of gasps and the stinging shouting of my name as they exclaimed: "Tsvia! What did you do?" I was mortified, and it took several months to get over my utterly sinful Bad.

For the most part, though, I thrived during those three years of my adolescence; but, more importantly, I got to know how other people lived, envying my friends' "normal" lives. They seemed to be intrinsically loved *unconditionally*! It made my eyes sing with want as I observed their civility and affection toward each other. I imagined how wonderful it would be to have loving parents: a pleasant dad who'd tell me I was pretty or even shake my date's hand, a mother and father who would hug me—nothing else.

But the chameleon had more colors to assume. I loved and did very well at both the Hebrew parochial school and at the high school, the Chicago Jewish Academy, which I attended for two years. In my junior year, my family, dissatisfied with the worsening neighborhood, once again moved, leaving the West Side for the North, and my life was once again abruptly roiled—from the lovely, spiritual, and insular Jewish cocoon to the snobby, sterile, upper-middle class universe of Senn High, a school as enormous and cold as a penitentiary, where one was judged by how many cashmere sweaters one had, and I had none.

That first year I spent many hours crying in the school's girls' room. I, who as a young girl, had stood up so confidently in classrooms, describing my dreams and having no problem making friends, was becoming self-conscious and developing a slight stutter. It may have started with my need to wear glasses to see the blackboard. One day the frame broke. Rather than buy a new pair, my mother taped the broken ends together, which often slipped and left me looking lopsided. I was standing up in class one afternoon, answering a question the teacher had posed, when in the middle of my recitation the glasses fell apart and hung by the tape on the tip of my nose. I think it was the laughter of my peers that erased all my youthful confidence and left me struggling.

Adding to my discomfort, I was *not* developing boobs. Most of my friends seemed to have sprouted them by junior year, but not me. So I stuck rolled-up socks in my little bra, except that, a couple of times, one slipped down while the other remained in place. Had to bag that! Then I heard about this new air bra that was guaranteed to make you look amply feminine. What you did was blow into a little straw they supplied, and when you inflated it to the desired size, you pulled the straw out, snapped the bra closed, and *voila!* Jane Russell!

I loved how voluptuous I looked and felt I had it going on at last, so when the school dance was on I mustered the courage to go to it and make Senn friends. I put on the bra, and I thought maybe it was working, because several boys asked me to dance. I was happily dancing with one when suddenly I heard a hissing sound! Need I say more? . . .

So I gave up and just slouched.

The junior year at Senn was so pathetically miserable that, whenever hear the line, popular then, "Put another nickel in, in the Nickelodeon," I cringe with discomfort.

SINGING LIGHT

IT'S NO SURPRISE THAT SONGS can bring you smack back to when you first heard them. "Saturday Night Is The Loneliest Night In The Week," and I'm right back in my late teens–early twenties, painting fake "nylons" with "seams" on my legs, putting talcum powder on my torso before wrenching into a torturous rubber girdle, and ironing my bras to make them pointier. "Chatanooga Choo Choo" or Shoo Fly Pie," and I'm younger than a teen, playing Pinners on the doorstep in front of my house, or "Red Rover Red Rover" or "Mother May I?" in the middle of the street. . .or singing, "We strolled the lane together," or "Mairzy doats" while roller skating all scabby-kneed, Mercurochrome-elbowed, having to stop every so often to tighten the skates with a key, and, bouncing balls, "'A' my name is Alice. . .and my husband's name is Alex," "Peg of My Heart." When I grew up and got married, I'd have three children, a boy and two girls, named Susan, Virginia, and Richard, and I'd be very special! Maybe I'd also be a scientist like Madame Curie or a beautiful movie star like Susan Hayward, but for sure I'd be very good and happy, as I promised myself in that tin mirror.

We saved fat in a used coffee can during the war to redeem coupons, and fake "margarine" we called Butterine that was white, so you had to squeeze a little tube of yellow into it to make it look more palatable. "Oh, Playmate, come out and play with me," and I'm younger yet, transported to kindergarten (only one of two other white kids (I had a penchant for eating clay), loving to dance to "How Do You Do, My Partner" with the kids, holding hands, prancing in a circle. (Spoiler alert: This self-indulgent nostalgia is going to continue a bit since I'm enjoying it, so you can skip two pages or so if you'd like.)

It was in first grade (so I was five) that I told my first joke, reciting it at Show and Tell time. "What is the difference between a plane and a baby? A plane goes from city to city, and a baby goes from titty to titty."

Going back further: "What you mean, Jelly Bean, just what I said, Chicken Head," "And they swam and they swam all over the dam!" when I'm not old enough for school, jealously watching my baby sister Dorothy nursing on Mother's breast. One time, Mother had eaten cabbage when she nursed Dorothy, and they both expelled gas! How I grew to hate Dorothy because she was not only adorable, with her big blue eyes and curls like mine, now getting all the attention, but because she was a real Robinson. (It would become patently clear as time went on that Eileen and I were not legitimate Robinsons, and we indeed felt every bit the stepchildren. Fast forward a few decades, and "Daddy," when he died, left a small fortune to Dorothy and Vivien and not a *sou* to Eileen or me...nor did my sisters have the class to offer any to us. But it was Dorothy I did play with the most, since Eileen shunned me, considering me a brat. Bored and if unable to find a playmate, I'd play School with Dorothy, placing her on a pillow next to some dolls, with me being the teacher and dead serious about it. Dorothy lapped up any attention I gave her. And I loved being Bossy Pants. Often we'd play "Maria LaJanna," a game I made up in which she was the star, Maria, and I was her assistant, Johnny. It was quite elaborate and went on for what seemed like hours until one of us got tired of it. She would also accompany me during my sweeping-the-stairs chore. Sometimes, taking a break, we'd sit on one, singing, "You'll never know just how much I love you" like

Alice Faye, with the "you-oo-oo-oo" and in such seriousness you'd have thought we were on a live stage. She was also company for me in my baby-sitting chores. For her I was the bones of fun. When our family went to nearby Michigan City for a summer vacation, our location was usually called "Stop Two" on that beach's road and near a park. One afternoon (if Vivien was one or so, Dorothy was five-ish, so I'd have been nine), it was my job to take my sisters for a walk in the park, pushing Vivien in the stroller with Dorothy hanging onto my hand or piece of my clothing. I vividly recall how I made lemonade out of lemons by turning the chore into a challenge. Resigned to having to babysit, I'd make up songs about the trees and the bees and the love from above, and the fun from the sun (hey, I was a kid!). Anyway, my audience of one ate it up! Baby Vivien was clueless about this budding Cole Porter!

Later that year, Vivien, at about age two, almost plunged to her death.

Mother often hung her wash on the roof of our building, us kids trailing her and amusing ourselves with playing Cat-in-the-Cradle hand games, singing songs, or whatever. That day, Mother had finished and started to walk down the little pull-down ladder, the one that conveyed us to the roof from a bedroom below. At the very moment she reached the downstairs floor, her phone rang. It was Aunt Min, who also lived in our building, in hysterics. Standing three flights down in the dairy yard, she'd heard a baby crying and looked up at our roof. Somehow Vivien had managed to crawl over to a small area of the roof where there was no protective wall and was sitting there crying, with her little legs dangling downwards toward the ground. In the split-second that my Aunt heard and saw her, I heard her too but couldn't see her for the hanging sheets. Being a child myself, I didn't know one shouldn't scream upon seeing their baby sister about to fall to her death, but when I cleared a sheet away and saw her, I did just that, to high heaven. But I was also fast enough to grab her in mid-air just as, startled by my own screams, Vivien turned, and, indeed, *was* about to fall! My mother, who had started to race back up the ladder, heard my screams and stopped, unable to move, sure it was too late. But there I came, a hero, clutching baby Vivien, still crying but all safe and sound. Mother says that was when her hair turned white.

 I saved Vivien another time, too. One beautiful day at the Michigan City, Indiana, cottage rental, situated steps from the sand dunes and the lake, I was standing on the edge of the water, trying to catch minnows in a pail, when I noticed a yellow scarf floating on the water—and discovered the scarf was attached to the head of little Vivien, who was sort of floating, head up, slightly under the water, her big brown open eyes staring straight up at me. Again, I was Mighty Mouse to the rescue! But nobody paid attention to me after I carried her to safety, so intent were they on getting the water out of her lungs. Vivien was seven lives short of being a cat! (The popular song at that time was "Would You Like To Swing on A Star"; I hear it, and I'm back there, Michigan City, Indiana, Stop Two.)

 If I hear Stardust—"Sometimes I wonder why I spend"—it's painful because that song was playing a lot during my (first) sleepover visit to Joan Cederborg, a friend from camp. I lived in the slums, and she lived in fancy suburban Winetka in a house straight out of a Hollywood movie set, complete with loving parents, a cute little brother she adored, and a cheery doting grandmother—oh, and a big fun dog. I loved her home, complete with a fire burning in the fireplace. Joan had a four-poster bed and pretty clothes. We had a fun day building a snowman, and that night her dad took us to a nearby frozen pond where we ice-skated in the moonlight and returned home all rosy-cheeked to a big cup of hot chocolate. I exaggerate you not.

I tell this because all the happiness turned into the worst pain of my life when her father, accompanying me to the train station so I could return back to Chicago, suddenly turned stern and asked if I had anything to tell him. When I demurred, to my horror, he looked in my suitcase and found the half bottle of Prell shampoo I'd stolen, along with a blue ribbon and a pencil from Joan's room. He asked why I would do such a thing. I don't remember anything else except that I cried uncontrollably the entire two-hour ride back home to the city, and, because I was so ashamed of myself, I risked my mother's wrath by confessing, but she surprised me by not punishing me and instead began giving me a small allowance. Ten cents a week. The grown-up me knows I just wanted a piece of Joan and her life, but that episode, at least obviating any potential road to larceny, still stings whenever I hear "Stardust."

Of course, smells can do that, too—transport a person.

Certain winter days under the right circumstances, by the smell alone, I'm seven or eight with my fellow students trudging into the Gladstone School, early morning before the first bell, our faces red with cold, exuding a combined scent of wet wool and rubbery galoshes amid hallways reeking of old wood, chalk, and sweat. Chicago winters were brutal, school mostly a chore.

A whiff of popcorn always elicits movies. I'm not yet a teen, it's Saturday afternoon, and I'm happy as a clam at high tide, standing with Eileen as we carefully choose which candy to buy with our precious nickels. She liked Chuckles, and I liked Milk Duds or Baby Ruth. Unable to wait, I'd inhale mine before we even sat down in the theater and then be slobberingly envious that Eileen had waited and beg her for some of hers. Maybe she'd give me the green piece, because she didn't like that one. Movies were (and in some small measure still are) my lifeline, penicillin against monotony. In those days, double features and the cartoon were fun, but you had to endure yucky *RKO Pathe News* with the crowing rooster, and they often showed boring President Roosevelt talking about the war, and, fidgeting on my seat, chewing on the end of my braid as was my habit, I'd stare at the bags under his eyes, praying it would be over soon, so we could finally see the picture. You knew they were scary movies if they were in black and white; musicals were all in color.

September to me is particularly distinguishable. Even today the unmistakable texture of the air and scent of September are uniquely identifiable. A whiff of burning leaves transports me back to grammar school. Rosh Hashanah. Special sun and shadows! There is an unmistakable light, which takes on a certain luster, casting longer shadows and, floating on currents of cooler air, instantly evoking the ambivalence I felt leaving our cottage in Michigan City.

September also brought a tinge of gratitude from me because

the long, hot, humid days were finally going, so maybe I could sleep nights (at the beach it wasn't so bad, but in the city some impossibly hot nights we'd actually go lie on the fire escape to try to get enough air—and be bitten to death by mosquitoes). Also, September signified maybe getting new shoes, black patent leather Mary Janes (you had to polish the scuffs with Vaseline), and though you didn't want to go to school, at least you had Halloween to look forward to. There's a song, "Spring Can Really Hang You Up the Most," which is true, but for me September doubles down in the nostalgia department.

If I hear "Just a Song at Twilight," I'm ten again, and my best friend Barbara Kranz's mother has died. They played that song at her funeral, my first, leaving an indelible impression on me, so that for years after I was unable to smell roses without being slightly nauseated. The song "Now and Forever," and I'm walking home from school for lunch, hearing on the radio the soap opera *Love of Life* (with Papa David and Chi-Chi) emanating from various houses, including my own, where Mother is making a lunch of salami and eggs with ketchup and rye bread.

Segueing to a blast from that past:

I have to give my mother credit for a clever way she handled a problem I was having in school. When we moved to the West Side and they enrolled me at the Gladstone Grammar School, I was maybe one of three white people in my class (substantiated by a picture of me in kindergarten), and we white kids got bullied a lot. It's plausible that my artistic ability protected me, though. Because my artwork was usually posted on the school walls, I had some small measure of popularity, or as the kids say, street cred.

Some schoolmates liked how I drew and insisted I "draw a girl" for them because, if I didn't, I'd get beaten up. So I did, and it saved me. Although I spent a lot of my youth terrified of getting beaten up, growing up among the poor kids had a lot of positive features. As I mentioned, I learned how to double-dutch jump rope and boogie-woogie. I could also climb the monkey bars in the playground as well as the best of them. One little friend, Gertrude, with her light brown skin, the longest eyelashes, and usually a faint odor of urine about her, was the most patient with me in her instruction. But colored Elizabeth (there were two Elizabeths in my class, and that was how we distinguished them) was not so patient and often menaced me by drawing her fists up to her eyes, whether I drew for her or not. I complained to my mother and, to my surprise, she told me to invite her over for lunch, which, I repeat, floored me. So I did. Sometimes my mother could be smart.

What I remember about that day was Elizabeth being quite polite and nice, appearing to enjoy her lunch. Two things struck me: one, her tongue was the same color as mine; and two, I worried whether the dishes would have to be especially scrubbed. I can only wonder what Elizabeth was wondering about me. By the way, any underlying prejudice I may have suffered under didn't preclude my flirting with Theotis, the cute black boy in the neighborhood. (Sitting on a stoop one day, he asked me if I wanted children when I grew up, and when I said I did, he asked, "Chocolate?") Anyway, my mother's ploy worked because, after that, happily, Elizabeth and I were cool, and I finally had a feathery sense of belonging.

Not only did my drawing save my little white tush, the dairy did as well. Situated behind our house (and the reason we there, remember), the dairy was mostly a chore for me. Literally. It was my duty to go there several times a week to fetch our milk, cream, butter, or cottage cheese, and such. After the first fascination, watching the milk dispensed into bottles along a conveyer belt, and how cottage cheese was made in a separate room (with its yucky smell), it became tedious having to go down three flights of stairs from our apartment to cross the yard, enter the dairy, get, and carry back the order. The bottles were cold and heavy. (The chore was also fodder for my nightmares because, in order to get to the freezer room where the milk was, I'd have to pass by the boiler room with its enormous, scary boiler that made loud monster fire sounds from inside.) Then I'd have to schlep all of the stuff back up those three flights of stairs. The stairs, however, did earn me the dime I'd need, along with two more pennies, to go to the movies on Saturdays, because that's what they paid me to sweep them twice a week.

In addition, I had to carry the garbage out daily to the smelly, fly-ridden alley cans behind our house. Not surprisingly, I hated chores, but the one I detested most was ironing. (I doubt if my children or grandchildren even know what an iron is! This is my definition of the epitome of unmitigated gloom: four o'clock, a cold March Tuesday, a pile of dress shirts to iron, and hours of homework to do.)

Another reason I got a pass from getting picked on, aside from drawing pictures, was that, on very hot summer days, I'd often sneak into the dairy, steal some little bottles of cold chocolate milk, and hand them out to my terrorists. At eight years of age, I was learning how to negotiate peace.

WHEN WAS I EVER AUTHENTICALLY ME AND NOT A CHAMELEON? I suspect that growing up without a good role model fed into this sense of being unanchored, along with a quick-change morphing ability. Some lucky people have, if not parents, substitute figures such as loving grandparents to be role models. That was not available to me since mine had died early in my life. I liked some uncles and aunts, but everyone lived far from everyone else. There were no great influential rabbis or teachers; therefore, movie stars became my role models. And they fluctuated from picture to picture— Lana Turner, Susan Hayward. The thing I ended up striving for and becoming, was, if not a movie star, at least an actress. I would become a great actress! Thus a *justified* chameleon.

SINGING LIGHT

Jack Shelton

THERE'S A CERTAIN ABSURDITY in the fact that, if it hadn't been for Sheldon Heller's hard-on, I never would have met Jack Shelton. Somehow that fact has crystallized as a marker in my life.

But Sheldon was horny and, at sixteen, I was a determined virgin. We had a terrible fight, broke up, and Mother, noticing me moping around the house, had a weak and rare moment of kindness, inviting me to go to the racetrack with her and her girlfriend.

It was there at the track that I promptly forgot about dying upon meeting a James Dean look-alike who was utterly sophisticated and manly, *completely* different from the stupid high school-fumbling, cheap-leather-jacketed, duckass-haired Sheldon Hellers, driving me to blatantly blurt out a lie when the first thing he said, upon approaching where I was standing at the gate, was "Only crazy people bet on horses."

"Yes," I said, "I think I'll stick to golf." I had never set foot on a golf course.

This effortlessly gorgeous guy, Jack Shelton, was not a kid but twenty-four! He had been to Europe, attended the University of Chicago with highest honors, and wasn't at all Jewish! And he did two unprecedented things in my life, starting with picking me up, and in time, proceeding to the other, God knew how, cramped inside his cute little MG. (The MG, a rarity in those early Fifties, provoked reactions from strangers, ranging from awe to "Aw" (this latter from a guy who stopped next to us at a stoplight): "Aw, whad'ja do, run out of flint?").

MOTHER AND I RARELY GOT ALONG. Our relationship was awash with adversarial complexity. She had a hair-trigger temper and no compunctions about taking her rage out on me. Ever defiant, I was determined not to "break," which enraged her more. I could be sixteen or seventeen, but it didn't stop her from beating me with her fists, a fly swatter, a mop. She once beat me so badly, accusing me of stealing some money she had left on the counter, that I was in my bedroom crying endlessly (and extra loudly so everyone would know my pain) when I heard Eileen come into the house and, outside my bedroom door, tell Mother, "By the way, I paid the delivery man with the money on the counter."

Mother later entered my room and declared, "I wasn't born a mother," her way of apologizing. When Jack Shelton came along, my new opiate, I wore him smugly like an invisible coat of armor and aimed him at her like a gun, impervious to her demands and threats to end the relationship with "the goy."

Surprisingly, a few months later, Mother didn't have a heart attack or beat me to death upon discovering my hidden diaphragm but, perhaps defeated or glad to get rid of me, insisted in no uncertain terms instead that I shit or get off the Jack. Since I hated living with my dysfunctional family, I was only too happy to trade Jacks. I laid it out to mine, and we got married that May after I graduated high school in January—the day before my eighteenth birthday. We left Chicago in our little MG, brimming with our records, books, clothes, and Trigger, our beagle, heading off for who knew where—just west! It was the most carefree time of my life.

AFTER CROSSING THE COUNTRY for an exciting yet scary three weeks, we arrived in San Diego, having lived on candy bars and water, saving what little money we had for gas and dog food. Jack had saved barely enough from working as a bartender while deciding what his calling in life would be. I had zilch and optimism.

We settled in Corona del Mar, since he'd gotten a job in nearby Laguna Beach selling foreign cars, and I worked as a secretary to help pay our rent. Though I'd vehemently protested in high school when mother insisted I take a secretarial course I considered boring, tedious, and pointless (since I intended only to be an actress), it came in handy and was small dues to repay Jack for emancipation and an education in Hip.

He opened my eyes, ears, and legs.

Eyes: Foreign film, how to shoot a rifle, what to read, be it Auden, Shakespeare, or Learned Hand. Ears: turning me on to Bartok, Berg, and Be-Bop. He taught me how to drink wine and scotch, and do pot. We occasionally dined in the best restaurants, where I actually ate frog's leg and snails (the girl who couldn't swallow soup!) even if it confined us otherwise to eating only hotdogs and beans for weeks on end because Jack so detested mediocrity (his credo was "It's okay to be lower or upper, but, my dear, *never* middle class!")

He was my Svengali, teaching me Meaningful Things, such as how, if man really wanted to, he had the ability to harness energy so that everyone in the world could have enough food to eat. He cautioned me about Non-Meaningful things, putting down the typical American woman who was buy me–give me–take me, as well as banks, parades, artificial plants, monograms, teaching dogs to do tricks, and behaving like the other typical American woman who didn't want or know how to fuck; and while he was at it, we did it everywhere, everyhow, morning, noon, and night—on an airplane, in a public restroom, elevators, the movies, doorways, in the snow laughing, "We're rich and drunk and twenty, and we shall never, ever die!"

And when he did it, it was like a rivet, a machine drill, *dut-dut-dut-dut,* almost hurting, but I pretended it was way groovy and, because he was my first and only lover, believed that was the way it was supposed to be, so I enticed, seduced, lap-danced, and thrust right back as we did it forward, backward, up and down, screaming out, not caring (probably liking) who heard, believing his hype that I was too much, something else, baby, while I drooled at his feet, sopping everything up, extolling him as Jesus on Earth, and totally grooving on our image that we were the coolest, sexiest couple, far more avant-garde and hipper than anyone breathing ever.

And then, coming up for air one morning four and a half years later, I awoke to realize I was tired of faking orgasms, that we had tried, experienced, felt, done, and said it all—that there was nothing left to say and most of it had been full of shit (on top of also suspecting him of an infidelity)—so all that was left to say was "Later," and that was it.

However, the Hail Mary for my failed marriage was that we were then situated in New Orleans.

HOW WE GOT THERE:

Early in our marriage while still in Corona del Mar, California, Jack found his "calling"—to be a psychoanalyst. But he needed to take some pre-med courses, so he chose Stanford and LSU medical school. (A genius with an IQ of 180, he could *choose* to go anywhere.) In New Orleans we lived in a room furnished with a mattress on the floor, an air-conditioner, his countless books, a card table, and two chairs, period. After a year, we moved to a cute, partially furnished shotgun apartment in the Quarter. I worked as a personnel manager at a department store, so he could do his premed. I worked five and a half days and, on the one Saturday afternoon I had free, volunteered as a Candy Striper at the hospital. It has been my life's habit to volunteer, "give back," for a cause, one way or another, but when I think about having only Sunday to myself—my only day to devote to cleaning and chores—I marvel at my energetic generosity.

I have this theory that people often unwittingly give away what they're thinking by the tune they're humming, which one can use to one's advantage. To illustrate, I'll jump years ahead. I'm playing poker with friends. It's a high/low game, and I'm competing with a player for the low hand, which, if I win, will give me the whole pot instead of splitting it. I have the coveted sixty-five, the penultimate best low but not a sure thing if he has the better sixty-four. Sweating little bullets as I decide which way to call the hand (I can easily claim the only high hand, guaranteed to win half the pot, or gamble on the low and possibly lose or win it all), I hear my opponent begin whistling the *Music Man* tune "Seventy-six Trombones." I call low, believing he has a seventy-six. He does, and I win it all. I give this as a preamble.

At around the time Jack and I had been married for four years, he started humming "You Are Too Beautiful," repeatedly singing one of its lines: "If on the other hand I'm faithful to you. . . ."

I suspected, and was proved correct, that Jack was starting a dalliance with the wife of a friend. No matter how much he denied, apologized, or beat his breast, protesting it was just flirtation, for me it was over.

Anyway, like a divine domino effect, each event morphing itself into the next, it was there in New Orleans that I met my *next* husband, Al Fisher, which then led to my soulmate, the man who would be my last husband for fifty-three years and who was probably why I'm still alive.

Had Sheldon Heller kept a cool tool, that is to say, I never would have met Al Markim.

IT'S A QUIRK OF MINE TO GRAB a moment in time and follow its thread to another arbitrarily monumental and seminal time as a direct result of it. Hence Sheldon Heller to Al Markim. Similarly, being a child who wanted to be an actress fed into the end of Jack

SINGING LIGHT

Shelton and the beginning of my true emancipation.

The one thing I had always wanted to be was an actress. My mother would tell how she enter what she thought was an empty house and hear lots of voices, only to discover it was eight-year-old Sondra looking in the bathroom mirror. Placing the bath towel around my body like a sarong and sashaying around, I was Dorothy Lamour declaiming to someone, or, with the towel draped over my head like a shawl, Maria Montez, a poor wretched soul pleading into the mirror to whoever, whatever. If I piled it high atop my head, I was Carmen Miranda ("Oh, *Chico, Chico!*"). Mother called me Sarah Heartburn. I remember once thinking I'd get some attention if I pretended I'd fainted, so I arranged myself on the floor, spreading my chenille robe just so and planting a pathetic, dead look on my face. When my mother saw me, did she fall to her knees, grab me, and cry out, "Oh, my poor darling, are you okay?" No, she just stepped over me and continued on her way. I hated that.

I believe that another reason I was drawn to acting was to overcome my deep shyness. I could then look in the mirror and not see the nebbish or shrinking violet I really was. I thought I wasn't pretty or smart or special in any way. Little could I have known that, years later, that plain jane would become attractive enough that she'd be dating two men a night (one at seven for dinner, and another at eleven for nightclubs!).

It was a given that my family would never help pay for me to go to college. Around the time I was about to graduate from high school and before I married Jack, I had a brief opportunity to pursue that dream. Eddie Smith—whom I never knew, having only been three when Mother left him—was the man everyone considered my father, including him. He had struck up a relationship with Eileen, who was by this time in her early twenties, and she convinced me to meet him, so, out of curiosity, I did. We actually met at a bar, and, though I wasn't of drinking age, I threw back a couple to assuage my nervousness and show him I was on equal footing. Probably the booze propelled an (apparently amusing) irreverence, because it seemed he liked me. My opinion of him, however, was not favorable. Gruff and tough, he looked like a more attractive version of Wallace Beery. I considered him another loser. But he did the one thing nobody in my life had—offer to help me financially, so I could pursue my acting career. I found a Chicago-based school, Columbia College, that specialized in all aspects of the new world of television. It didn't cost that much, but I was penniless, and Jack Robinson wasn't going to help, so I seized the chance with deep gratitude. Eddie didn't *know* I wasn't his, so what the hell! It was wonderful for about two months, until I told him I'd met and fallen for Jack Shelton. "A *goy?*" Eddie declared flat out, like my mother. "It's college or the goy."

That was the end of my great white hope of a career.

I married Jack the day before my eighteenth birthday in May. Comparing myself then to my equivalent-aged grandchildren now is mind-boggling.

We left Chicago to go out west, eventually to Stanford, where I worked as a secretary to support us. I also tried out for a part I got in the school's rather elaborate production of *Anything Goes*, which was being directed by a student, Warner Leroy (the son of Mervin Leroy, a big deal Hollywood producer. Warner one day became famous in his own right as the New York City restauranteur of the Russian Tearoom and Tavern On the Green.) That acceptance was no small achievement. I had the distinction of being the only non-student ever allowed to participate. When I first stepped out on that stage, I knew I was where I belonged. I totally tripped out with joy over the whole gestalt—the wolf whistles, laughter, and applause. My first taste! Manna! *Yes!*

When we moved to New Orleans for Jack's medical training, I tried out and got some parts in the little theaters, but the pickings were slim.

I was about twenty when I had the chutzpah to march into WDSU, New Orleans' major television station, decked out in a slinky white knit dress, big falsies, a saucy black beret on my long, and bleach-blonde hair, and ask for the entertainment director. Miraculously I was directed to Herman Livewright, to whom I announced, "I'm a singer" (not mentioning the venue of my performances was my shower). Long story short, I was given a tryout for a new comic from Indiana who they'd just hired. He was planning to put on a little variety show and was looking for a good-looking female singer. That man was Dick Van Dyke, who immediately liked and hired me on the spot. But, alas, the gig didn't last long, since he soon accepted an irresistible offer to do *Bye Bye Birdie*, leaving Sondra to say Bye Bye to her short-lived singing career. (Fifty years later, my husband Al and I ran into Van Dyke at a Malibu restaurant. I asked if he remembered WDSU, blah-blah, adding, "You went to New York to do *Bye Bye Birdie,* and," I quipped, pointing to my husband, "I went to New York to do him!").

At the end of the yoga classes I teach, I give little contemplations. There are two that still resonate: "When you lose, learn the lesson," and "Pain happens; suffering is optional." Scoff if you will, and, if you are like the younger me, it probably won't serve you. But how true those truisms are for me now!

Of the three bleakest periods of my life, the most catastrophic was the last one. I'll grapple with that later. But the grains of wisdom in those corny aphorisms served me then and do even now.

I was twenty-one when Jack Shelton and I were kaput. Penniless and stranded in New Orleans, far from family or good friends, it can't be overstated that it strained my naturally optimistic self. My job as a personnel manager—read: glorified secretary—for a department store barely covered expenses, the biggest being rent for our French Quarter shotgun apartment. I took it over, partially furnishing it the best I could.

Beside the bed, card table, and two metal chairs, I had end tables, candelabras, and shelves made of gold-painted cardboard, courtesy of my buddy the display manager at the department store. I also had custody of our Siamese cat, from whom, poor creature, I desperately tried sucking succor because I lived in a sea of insecurity. According to the psychoanalyst I'd been seeing, I was rife with "free-floating anxiety." My default remedy seemed to be lovers, who were anything but. Like a baby frantically sucking on an empty nipple, I inhaled men. If nothing else, they bought dinners, and I was dirt poor. My refrigerator typically contained milk, bread, wine, and gifted champagne. I was living on coffee, four packs of cigarettes a day (but I didn't smoke them to the bottom), and my saturation point for booze was the eighth scotch. I dated twelve men during that period and slept maybe four hours on a good night. So meals, basically, were courtesy of dinner dates. It's a mystery how I kept my job on four hours of sleep a night and hangovers every morning. There was a nightery in New Orleans called the 1-2-3 Club, which was open 24/7. I knew it was time to go home when the sun came out. It boggles my mind now, but think *Mad Men*, the television show, an accurate depiction of life in the Fifties.

It was during that dystopian period that I tried washing Jack out of my body's memory with new men. I became an angry thrill-junky. Jack had been my only lover, and it may sound contradictory, but I wanted to retrieve that faithful status by finding a new improved, kinder Jack, thereby generating a sort of Men as Band-Aids modus operandi. As I write these words, I am aware they may sound as if I thought I was the only person who ever dissipated and screwed up their youth. No. But I seemed incapable of getting off of the self-destructive trampoline I was on. This was Black Time Numero Dos.

I call it the black time because I was pathetically and systematically throwing me away.

Al Fisher

SO THERE I WAS—stuck in New Orleans, supporting myself at the department store and doing a few acting gigs. These were the lamentable circumstances when I found myself at Papa Joe's, a favorite haunt, a divorcée and wasted old soul at the grand old age of twenty-one. I can only describe my brain then as in a calcified state with a constricted ability to think beyond my immediate needs and its attendant triage need to overcome desperation.

I was slouched over the bar, joshing with acquaintances and having a "taste" or two, or four, when, entering stage right—and right in so many ways— in swaggered Al Fisher. If Jack Shelton was James Dean, blondish and beautiful, albeit in a slightly feminine way, here came Cornell Wilde, dark, masculine, more mature (sixteen years older than me) and Jewish, the antithesis of Jack. Unfortunately, he was not as brilliant, but that night at Papa Joe's he wooed me, coming on like gangbusters, mostly impressing me because I liked how smooth yet very uncomplicated he was. (Eventually I'd come to love how he loved me, so refreshingly easily and differently from Jack.) He had a way of squinting as he talked. Over another drink, he went on about how he'd seen me around, had been wanting to meet me but I was always with some guy, that I was yada beautiful, yada sexy, and on top of it all, yada Jewish. After some more back and forth, I was clearly boozed out. It was past time for me to go home. Seeing how inebriated I was, he insisted on accompanying me through the perilous New Orleans streets. The thing that really impressed me about him was, when we got to my place, I asked him in (no doubt with intentions to add another notch to my non-exclusive lover man's club); but, after somewhat undressing me and putting me in my bed, he told my closed eyes and opened arms, "No. I want you when you know it." That blew my mind, jarring me back momentarily to the real Sondra and not the new throwaway version I'd become.

As he left I remember asking him to turn off the light, to which he replied, "That's the sun!"

IT WAS THE FIRST TIME ANY MAN courted me the way he did, showering me with gifts and lavish attention. His first of many gifts was a gold ankle bracelet with the words *shaina punim*, which is Yiddish for "beautiful face." But his main gift was retrieving the decent person I had once been.

The other was getting me pregnant.

Not long after courting me, I moved in with him and, for the first time in ages, felt calm and safe. In a double ceremony with his best friend Abe, I became Mrs. Al Fisher. Fifteen months later our son was born.

I had wanted a child but had great doubts of ever achieving that because from the time I first got my period at age fifteen it only came once a year. There were obvious advantages to not having to deal with birth control or monthly menstruation, but at some point in my adulthood I consulted a gynecologist: I thought it prudent to find out why. He found that I had an "almost infantile womb," which would correct itself when and if I ever became pregnant, and it explained why, thankfully, I never had. When Al Fisher and I decided to try for a baby, the doctor gave me some shots, which he claimed might help me become fertile. My psychoanalyst, with whom I was just finishing up, also took credit for me becoming pregnant, claiming my problems were psychological and that I'd worked them through. (Somewhat earlier, while married to Jack, I had entered therapy because Jack was going to be a psychoanalyst and it was protocol for wives of psychoanalysts to undergo analysis. By the way, as the wife of a medical student, the fee was three dollars a session!) Ostensibly, that is why I saw the shrink, but the truth was I was actually, in spite of the prolific sex, quite frigid in my marriage with Jack, courtesy of. . .pick a Jack. Robinson? Shelton?

Doctors be damned; when, after a year of trying and the pregnancy was at last successful, ironically, nobody gave Al Fisher credit! But he was caring, quite a good lover, and obviously effective!

Interestingly, when I did learn of the pregnancy, who do you think was the third person I told? If you guessed Jack Shelton you're right. I marched straight to the med school, full of hubris, found him in the auditorium and hurled my news at him: Take that!

My marriage with Al Fisher lasted as long as my previous one—four and a half years. Why I left Fisher isn't pertinent to my story except to say that marrying on the rebound never was a good idea. It's clear I considered one of Al's best assets simply that he wasn't Jack Shelton. I soon learned other things not too wonderful about him as well. As a salesman, he was able to support us okay but he had this thing about "putting on the dog," giving the impression he was bigger, richer, and better than he was, such as taking a wad of small bills and wrapping a one-hundred dollar bill around them, or giving me a six-carat "diamond" engagement ring made of zircon. To me the final straw was coming out of a theater one evening after seeing *La Strada*. I was so choked up with emotion I couldn't speak when he groused, "What the hell was that crap about?" I knew then that it was over. It never should have begun.

But at twenty-four, I had my dignity back and my son Gary, and for that I will never regret, and forever be grateful to, Al Fisher.

Al Markim

DIRTY WORKS AT THE CROSSROAD, OR TEMPTED, TRIED AND TRUE was the name of the melodrama I performed and starred in on the River Queen, an old steamer packet showboat moored on the Mississippi River. My role was Ida Rheingold, the villainess with a heart of gold but a lost soul who, in the last act, is saved, chaste and redeemed. That came at the tail end of my marriage to Al Fisher.

Keep your finger on the place.

Lest we dismiss those four years, life as Mrs. Al Fisher had ensconced me quite pleasantly in a community circle of affluent Jewish people. I'd joined groups like Hadassah (even singing and performing in some of their entertainment benefits). I also shopped, played cards, and shared kiddie stories with my well-heeled women friends, and went out to dinner with them and their husbands regularly. I had the means to take better care of myself—eating and sleeping regularly, and attending to my hair, nails, and clothes.

I found myself socially sought after and knew this time it wasn't, as in the past, just for my looks or body.

But on that score, I need to address the issue more fully. I readily admit I disagree with those who claim the high ground and denigrate the importance of beauty. My own truth is quite different. For me, appearance was the great equalizer. In fact, I felt privileged to live and thrive within the male gaze of approval. Blessed or cursed with it, my looks served me well for many years until, like a warm blanket removed, age rudely cashed me out. After all, what do you do if you haven't got wealth, support, position, great genius, or athletic talent? My looks opened doors otherwise closed to a person with no other resources. (Even if those doors turned out to be revolving ones or flimsily screened, it seemed to me, I had no other options.)

To set the scene of this stage of my life then, I must preface the following with a disavowal of false modesty. I am an old woman now, no longer in possession of my youthful looks. I'm not coy, so the only to describe my life then, eschewing braggadocio, is give an example of how those doors opened for me.

My twenties were a heady time. One afternoon while I was walking in the city, an ogling motorist, not paying attention, slammed into the car in front of him. It wasn't the only time that happened. Being an old person now with a body that could benefit from a good iron, I don't deny enjoying having once been pretty enough to cause accidents, so I say a big whoop for prettiness!

Also, nearly sixty years ago, when I was a proverbial big fish in a little pond (albeit the Mississippi River), and rather full of myself, I began to take my small measure of fame for granted: my picture in magazines, constantly in the papers advertising "Sondra Invites You on the *River Queen*," a gossip columnist for the *Times-Picay*une (the "Lagniappe") extolling, "That luscious redhead who looks like Rita Hayworth sashaying in the Blue Room, Sondra Fisher," people asking for my autograph, and, standing smack dab in front of the entrance plank to the boat, an eight-foot cardboard picture of me in my scanty costume, arms outstretched. As popular as I was becoming, I believed then that it was just a stepping-stone to a glorious career to come. (Instead, it would be the highlight.)

In agreeing to divorce, Al and I decided that I would stay at our little house on Catina Street with toddler Gary and a live-in baby-sitter. He kindly offered to move to Colorado, where a pal of his offered solace, a job in his restaurant, and a place to stay.

It didn't take long in our tight community for word to get out that I was newly single and available. Abundant numbers of men seemed to appear out of the woodwork and, having felt enchained by two marriages so early in my life, I was hungrily free to receive them, looking for Mr. Right. But those seeds of seduction were heaped on me prematurely. I learned what I needed to survive and thrive, took that ball, and ran with it, sometimes into a wall, sometimes not. Having discovered this dubious power, I would have been a fool not to exploit it. Men flocked to me like moths to flame, as mentioned, sometimes two dates a night—all the while I smoked four packs of cigarettes a day and guzzled my usual eight scotches. Although I had cleared my name, I hadn't quite cleared my game. I must reiterate, though, that as much as I was a shameless tease and indulged in heavy petting, I did not go "all the way" lest I get a bad reputation, which I didn't want to risk sullying again. This *was* the Fifties and early Sixties. And the moral paradigm of that era was nothing like it would become in subsequent ones.

Like the character in the book *Candy* who was always being hit on—I'm not proud to say (probably I was sending out some weird vibes) that it seemed as though every person I met made a move on me, including a woman or two. Astonishingly, they included my trusted gynecologist and my psychoanalyst (granted, I was no longer his patient when he hit on me, but he must have known it wouldn't further my self-esteem). And there were various bosses I'd worked for, and unsurprisingly, many people in show biz, including a big deal Hollywood director (who, because I was bored with the endless hours of standing around a set doing nothing—as well as what I perceived as the indignity of being just a bit actor—I almost wanted to screw to get *out* of the picture). There was the head announcer at WDSU, who would surreptitiously announce he loved me when he gave the broadcast time: "This is WDSU New Orleans, it's nine p.m. Longovongee," (which was how time was done in those days.) That was code for "love," hastily added and apparently never noticed, except by me. Our code language consisted of taking the letters of a word you wanted to say in secret and adding "ong" between each consonant: L(ong), O, V(ong), E. I got a childish kick out of his announcing his professed love for me to the station's world, even if they didn't know it.

My next-door neighbor was a French count named Jacques de la Verne. I hesitate to mention him because his relationship with me stretches credulity. Adoringly, he had observed my marriage with Jack Shelton and the fights therein, his puppy dog eyes oozing sympathy, so that, when the marriage ended, he offered to take me on a holiday to recover. I accepted with the caveat that there would be no *quid pro quo*—and he kept his word! We actually shared a hotel room in Haiti where I spent a few days enjoying myself tremendously. I never knew whether he was impotent, gay, or merely honorable, but he kept his word. I loved the island, and it was there that we went to a voodoo where I was the only white woman and had to drink from a community bottle of potato vodka that burned my lips before touching them. (I faked drinking it.)

Then there was Walter, a fantastic adventurer and Ernest Hemingway look-alike, who owned a yacht, lived half the time in Tahiti, constantly exclaimed how fabulous Tahitians were, and bestowed upon me the supreme compliment that I was like one of their women. He said I was "childlike," not childish, but a free spirit, like them. He and his matriarch wife, Enid, had a big home centrally located in the Quarter, a sort of main drag for any and everyone, important or not. In the evenings, serving big jugs of burgundy wine, they'd play Tahitian music, pass out *pareus* (sarongs) for us to wear while dancing—and dance we did, in wild, alcohol-fueled abandon. People from wandering tourists to cute young Tulane students would gawk at us through the opened doors, and often joined us. I adored Enid because she was erudite, an educator, and a wonderfully motherly woman who seemed wowed by my cache of Jack Shelton-learned poetry. Yet being morally untethered, I felt little compunction about enjoying her husband constantly trying to put the moves on me. I'm not condoning it, but one needn't be a shrink to decipher the underlying dynamics. (I will not continue to try justifying being a serial tease. If I could go back and recalibrate, I'd do it in a New York heartbeat. But it's useless to—as today's kids say—"throw shade" at it, because it was what it was. Clearly, my higher self had flat-lined; no use defending it.) But, to quote Omar Khayyam, "The moving finger writes and, having writ, moves on." Moving right along. . . .

Most of the men I dated were single, but all of the ones mentioned above were married. I didn't care. They kept me occupied, flattered my needy ego, and fed my hungry gut. In my mind, I wasn't a threat to their marriage because of my celibate policy. (One exception, R., the head honcho of the River Queen, though also married, had a deeply serious case on me. He left his wife and children in the mistaken hope I would love him in return, no matter how much I tried to dissuade him. It gave me pause, but in my state of mind then, I brushed it off as Oh Well.) And Jacques de la Verne's wife had also tried to seduce me, so I dismissed that involvement as well.

And there was the extremely wealthy man I knew who could have ended all my financial woes. He even offered to keep me, but he just didn't turn me on. (The one thing I recall is that he had a valet whose name was Joe Green—*How Green Was My Valet*, I punned.)

I managed to go out with all these men without actually consummating our relationships, though I came close enough—lots of heavy making out, and my "no" had a comma, not a period, attached to it, keeping them hoping, but I was saving my newly refurbished butt for Mr. Right. I didn't want to repeat sinking down the same rabbit hole I'd suffered after the first marriage fiasco.

Thinking about it now, I realize many of my men friends surely guessed I was just blowing smoke with my tale of virtue. I'm truly surprised at how they seemed content with just hugs and kisses, but I surmise they were waiting for the right opportunity to finally score.

That's what I was thinking when I made an exception and went to bed with Al Markim. He was from out of town, knew nobody, so, in a town with wall-to-wall *yentas*, nobody would know.

But I'm getting ahead of myself.

Good gigs were not that plentiful in New Orleans, so one grabbed what one could. Besides acting on the boat and in a few local theaters, I had a bit as a dancer who wiggled her tush as the foil for the quasi-famous comic, Jackie Kannon, who performed at the Roosevelt Hotel's Blue Room nightclub. I also did a stupid independent film called *The Frigid Wife* (my part being the hot one of course), and a nonspeaking role in a better Hollywood movie, *A Walk On the Wild Side*, with Jane Fonda, Lawrence Harvey, and the French actress Capucine.

Partnering with that talented announcer at WDSU, we put on a radio show we called *Omnibus to Nowhere,* a poor man's Mike Nichols and Elaine May bit. I did countless voice-overs and, on live TV, some clothes modeling as well as representing a segment called "The Play Lady" who read children stories. Also there was that short-lived stint on the *Dick Van Dyke Show*. Meantime, all the while, I was trying to be a good mother to my little boy with the help of a babysitter/housekeeper whom I paid twenty-five dollars a week, and it cost four dollars for a laundress on Thursdays.

That was what things cost in those years, and while I'm at it I'd like to add a plug for me: The reason people (at least I) married so frequently then was that the moral ethos of the time demanded it; now, unmarried people just live together.

THEN I GOT THE *RIVER QUEEN* BREAK. Picture this: The boat, last of the famous steamer packet boats, was in itself a beauty: majestic, romantic-looking, all lit up and bedecked with welcoming flags cheerily waving in the balmy breeze. The January evening when Al Markim came aboard was spectacular, complete with a fabulous sunset. Weather in New Orleans can often be oppressively hot and the humidity almost insulting, sometimes so bad that a person can't even fight with her husband, and making love could be an embarrassment of slippery, sweaty sounds that almost stopped you but you had to laugh.

That temperate January night was perfect and, along with a buxom blonde from Georgia the mayor had arranged as a date, Al Markim—eager for a fun evening—climbed the plank.

Greeted on the first level to the sound of the great New Orleans musicians Al Hirt and Pete Fountain playing New Orleans-style music, drinks were served before going below to the theatre. People started to relax enough to respond to the serenade of scents—a hint of chicory coffee from the nearby Café du Monde mixed with the next-door Jax Brewery's beery aromas, along with a *frisson* of magnolia blossom, all tempered by the river brine itself and friendly, Southern-mannered people joking and laughing in a prelude to a very pleasant evening, if you discount a mosquito bite or two.

New Yorker Al Markim, at thirty-four, an urbane, good-looking, successful businessman, worked in the entertainment field, primarily video and television. Very unlike me, he had an impeccable moral compass, save for one testosterone-driven caveat: He had a zipper problem. His code of ethics permitted him to cheat on his wife if he was "out of town." Like a Get Out of Jail Free card, it wouldn't count!

I could rationalize and perhaps explain how, as a teenager, he had been madly in love with Sylvia, his college sweetheart and fiancée who, one November, asked him to feel a lump in her armpit and in January was dead, and how, out of this grief, he met a woman he married too soon. But this is an explanation, not an excuse. Perhaps he shared the weakness of many men dictated to by their groins, unable to be satisfied with only one woman. Yet in all other respects, and certainly in business, his reputation was impeccable. His word was gold, a handshake enough of a contract, and in every other way he was a paragon of virtue.

He came to New Orleans scouting for a June Allyson commercial. He had been told by the mayor to catch the show on the boat because it was a hoot. So with a fellow businessman and that pretty blonde woman draped on his arm, Al Markim came aboard, primed to let those good times roll, quite unprepared for what would turn out to be one of the biggest things that ever happened to him.

SINGING LIGHT

To We Or Not To We

MY VERSION: THERE I WAS, CHILDREN—a star! On a stage! While Dad sat in the audience at one of the large beer kegs-cum- table, like a stage-door Johnny. He was so impressed with my great acting that he sent a note backstage asking if I'd join him in the lounge after the show.

His version: Yeah, I was impressed. . .with her legs.

When I saw that note, I was stoked by the hope that maybe these big-deal *machers* from New York wanted to offer me a part in their production. My fellow cast members were almost as excited for me as I was as I rushed up to the lounge, drenched in perfume and anticipation, and calculating the effect my auburn hair and heavily made-up jade eyes would have—draped in an almost-real fur leopard jacket thrown insouciantly over my outfit, a black cashmere turtle neck sweater, black tights, and spiky heels.

He was sitting with his cohort, a dark-haired man named George Gould, along with the pretty blonde from Georgia whose ample boobs seemed to dominate the table and whose name I instantly forgot.

Over a cigarette and brandy, sneaking a glance, I thought his looks were cool enough, though I usually preferred dark- haired men and had initially aimed those eyes at George, but no one was home there. The Markim guy had a sort of affable macho thing going. He had a nice build, with full, quick-to-smile lips and silky, wavy hair the color of wet sand. But mostly, I liked how his pale green eyes—so similar to mine—conveyed a keen projection of intelligence and steadily held one's gaze, unwaveringly direct in a down-to-earth way. Initially he intrigued me because he struck me as quite sophisticated, a contradiction to his getting-down hominess, such as telling a couple of witty jokes with perfect delivery (reminding me of my roots), so refreshingly un-Southern; an alchemy of urbanity and *haimishness*. And though he came off as a perfect gentleman, I couldn't fail to notice his eyes trying me on for size.

The first serious thing I said to him, God knows why, was, "You look like me." I wasn't referring to physical resemblance, but to the fact that, somewhere behind his eyes, I saw me. Home. I couldn't explain it then and can't now.

The second seminal thing that happened was, while dancing with him on the nearby floor, I told him, "Get rid of Peaches."

Initially I was disappointed that, upon meeting, instead of getting down to business and offering me an audition, he was ho-hum, just coming on to me. As if the blonde wasn't even there, he had quickly asked me to dance. My first reaction was that he wasn't my type. It took but a few steps to feel a certain mojo creeping over me in his firm arms, digging how confidently he led. Eyelashes brushing against my cheek, he said I reminded him of high school. When I asked why, he explained I smelled of grease paint (so much for my fab perfume) and went on to explain he'd also been an actor, starting in high school. Settling comfortably in his arms, I asked if he was married. "Happily so," he said, "with three wonderful children." Since I was not a paragon of rectitude, I didn't judge him but, taking that in and recalling how R., the manager of the boat, had recently left his wife and children for me, I jokingly cautioned, "Well, watch out for me—I'm a home wrecker!"

Perhaps we danced some more, but eventually we sat at a separate table talking. The exact choreography now escapes me. I do recall admiring his intelligence and cordiality, as well as feeling some vague stirrings that maybe he'd be someone I could get real with, including in bed, because, to repeat, he was safe: happily married, out of town, knowing nobody in my social circle, he'd never tell, and he'd just go away back to New York. It would be bang-bang, thank you, sir. What I do know for sure, the overwhelming vibe and alchemy between us was extraordinary. It was something new. The word that best describes it, I now realize, is *thrilling*!

One of the most compelling things resonating in me was the way he seemed to really listen to me instead of chomping at the bit in a hurry to say what *he* was thinking. Rather than offering the usual verbal fillers, he spoke about substantial things, asking me about myself, career, relationship to my son, etc. Also I loved how his eyes said things not said. It was implicit we were "getting" each other.

Accustomed to being a dazzler, I began to feel dazzled. Among other things, he seemed much smarter than me, and I was unable to predict the next thing he was going to say as I usually could with most men. Within a short time, he was outwitting and deliciously entertaining me. I loved that. I wanted more. The problem, however, was my safety plan that he'd be temporary and a one-night-stand was double-edged. I was attracted to him enough to consider sex, but I also liked him enough to want his respect and for him to get to know me seriously. Which, paradoxically, is why I refused his advances—and it would take a year until I didn't.

Returning to New York with a promise he'd keep in touch left me with a tinge of sadness, but I soon returned to my busy life, chalking him up to Oh Well.

It wasn't long before I started getting the first of his many letters, which was how I got to know him better. The more I did, the more I liked him—and got sucked into the vortex of his astounding mind and personality. I began looking forward to the mail as a child does Christmas.

Inheriting the wealth of loving parents, Al was the first generational and only son of Julius and Jean, who lived in Wilkes-Barre, Pennsylvania. He was that rare person (to me, anyway) with an actual happy childhood. He was seven years older than me, also a Depression baby, but what his parents lacked in money they made up for in joy of life and sheer humanity. They inculcated in him the belief he was a winner (which carried him throughout his life). He never felt poor because, for one thing, all his friends were too, and his parents made the best of it with good humor. He made skis out of curtain rods and, at the age of six, showed his entrepreneurial talent by charging his buddies two cents to see his new baby sister, Renee. Although he maintained a great appreciation for his Judaism, he was basically an atheist who abided by the Ten Commandments (or, if you want to be picky, the Nine).

During World War II, when he was seventeen, he patriotically enlisted in the army. In Germany, he met the renowned director Arthur Penn, who encouraged Al to pursue an acting career. He described some bad experiences—in particular, being a Jew among non-Jews. But a highlight he often spoke of fondly occurred when, because he was a journalist for his Company and they sent him to cover the Nuremberg trials, he sat right there just feet away from major war criminals like Hermann Goering and Albert Speer. It was the tail end of the war, so he was fortunate not to encounter any real fighting and came home unscathed, a hero to his family.

In the early 1950s, only in his twenties, Al played the role of "Astro," regarded as the prototype for *Star Trek*'s Mr. Spock, and he one of the stars of a popular children's television program called *Tom Corbett, Space Cadet,* which brought him a great deal of fame and recognition. He studied at the Actor's Studio under the great theatrical teacher Irwin Piscoter, along with Marlon Brando and Harry Belafonte. Among his numerous stage and screen roles during the 1950s, he performed in *The Adventures of Superman* and on the Philco-Goodyear Television Playhouse's *Love of Life*; he co-hosted Jerry Lewis Muscular Dystrophy marathons and co-starred in *La-Ronde* at the Circle in the Square Theatre. (Amusingly, at the time, a young wanna-be actor named George Segal, who admired Al and would sweep his dressing room, went on to become an important A actor. When he asked Al's advice on becoming an actor, Al told him to give it up, that he'd never make it. Luckily Segal didn't listen to him!)

Al eventually got tired of being an actor or, as he put it, "just a pawn." He would later get involved in film producing and then become a pioneer in the new medium of video entertainment, but at the point we met, he was producing television commercials for a company acquired by MGM.

His marriage to a pretty blonde named Gladys Schnautzer, whom he met while a student at the New School, where she worked in an office there (and whom he renamed Billie), produced three children, Nancy, Dan, and Nina, approximately three years apart. When Al and I met, they'd been married ten years or so. He claimed they never once had a single fight and coexisted like very compatible roommates.

In a short while, as I was getting to know Al better, it felt as if I had exchanged my Cinderella hat for Goldilocks's: Having found Mr. Just Right, I'd hit the jackpot. He was not only smart like Jack Shelton but not at all neurotic. He was kindhearted and Jewish like Al Fisher—but, unlike him, extremely mature and a person of phenomenal character. Still the stubborn fact remained that, as much as I felt enchanted by him, it wasn't my intention to get seriously involved with (a) a married man, and (b) one with three children. I was only in my twenties, had learned my lesson from two marriage mistakes, and wasn't about to make another. And yet, and yet. . .shamelessly carrying my fairy-tale metaphor further, I was beginning to feel like the female equivalent of Pinocchio, unable to withstand temptation by staying on the righteous path.

I believe that, had we not lived apart, requiring the need to write to each other, we probably never would have fallen in love. Correction: We didn't *fall* in love. It was more like we were captured! But it was through those handwritten words, those love letters, that magic began to weave us together.

IT TOOK PRACTICALLY A YEAR before Al could manufacture a reason to return to New Orleans. On a sunny, cool October day, our first date was a football game at Tulane, with me pretending I liked football.

Our first night together was *stunning*. How to describe the rush I felt? I can't. It was a game-changer in both our lives, and it set in motion our forever. But I won't tarnish its memory by attempting to explain it. I'm insufficient to the task. Everything I could say has already been said by poets and people far better and more talented than me.

We were stuck. I guess we hadn't gotten the memo, because he unquestionably hadn't asked to land in such a predicament. He had genuine affection for his wife, and when I asked him what was wrong with her, he said it was the sin of *omission,* not *commission*. His children were everything to him. Naming the most important things in life, he'd have listed his children first, then work, then family (which encompassed his wife and nuclear one), then the Yankees, more or less in that order. He wasn't a token father. He was a hands-on one, even wanting and making the formula for the babies, an arduous and tedious task in those days. As an actor he often had plenty of free time to devote to taking care of their first-born, Nancy, and he did an exemplary job of it, taking her for daily walks and to school, and so on. Incidentally a beautiful baby, she appeared on television and was one of the faces of the Gerber baby. (Both Nancy and Danny earned money appearing in television commercials.) When Danny was born, Al was beside himself with joy, only too happy to have a son to play ball with, taking great pride in his "Daniel Maniel," as he jokingly called him. Little Nina, the "mouse", as a cute little toddler, learned how to do math by accompanying him in the bathroom where, sitting on the john, he'd use the printed animals on the wallpaper to create math games.

And I *certainly* didn't want to deal with his baggage or its ensuing guilt. He didn't belong to me—we'd met too late. Yet although it was abundantly clear we were in over our heads, good-bye was not in our vocabulary.

I remember a good friend cautioning me, "Sondra, you cannot build happiness on someone else's unhappiness." Ya think? Believe me, I got that. I also get that *owning up to something is not always enough*. I also get that I didn't take him from her. I *found* him. But the unadulterated truth was it was too late to Rewind or Undo. (I hasten to add, some time later the same girl friend told me, "It's clear your love is made in heaven.")

The following year, sinking deeper into the quicksand, we grabbed our moments whenever he could manufacture reasons for a trip to Louisiana. Sometimes I'd have to meet him in Baton Rouge or some other place. There was a whole lot of fucking and crying (goodbyes at airports). My plan to just have a casual sexual relationship had gone *pffft* into a full-blown love affair, leaving me hoist by my own petard. Any "us" had zero future because, as he had made abundantly clear, he would never leave his children. I would have to be his mistress, and my need for a soul mate–husband, as well as a father for my son and any future children, was simply not on the table.

Helpless to end it, our "arms round the griefs of the ages," this went on for some time.

AND THEN IT DIDN'T. CONTROL. ALT. DELETE. Gambling—I finally mustered the nerve to say I'd had enough. The situation had become too unacceptable, too unfair to me *and* Billie. He had to make a decision then and there.

After a heart-wrenching pause, he did. Swing and a miss— that was the end of any happily ever after for me. Devastated, my only request was he not try to reach me ever again. *La commedia e finita!*

And this time it was crying but no fucking. Unable to fault my wishes, Al gallantly if reluctantly accepted them and made the hard decision. It left me like a cat trying to heal its wounds by crawling under a bed and wallowing in self-pity. I felt life had stopped— but I was still a mother and still had a job, and in time I willed myself to get back on the horse. I also returned to my default hobby of collecting men's affections. But this time, crushed, angry, and throwing my reputation to the winds, it was not just for their affection: I would no longer be alone in my bed.

It's conceivable that the me of then, seriously scathed by my past, suffered some sort of psychiatric disorder that needed attention but wasn't getting it. But our national moral paradigm from the late Sixties on was nothing like it had been earlier. A person alive in the late Fifties early Sixties, inclined to judge, would have considered my behavior—my flirting—utterly slutty. Maybe it was. The promiscuity was twisted enough. These days, such behavior is more often than not met with, "So what else is new?"

Among my boyfriends was the entertainment director of the Playboy club, a sexy, Italian, and talented musician named Al Belletto (*another* Al! A name I don't even like, though admittedly it made the love-cooing transition easier!). With him I drowned my sorrow with alcohol, good jazz, and weed. It was also a gas, as we'd say, to participate in the club with all the bunnies—in particular on New Year's Eve, when just before midnight they'd gather the bunnies in a room apart from the rowdy, horny, drunk men for a half hour or so. I joined them, heard some choice tales of their experiences, and was really grooving on them until one bunny said "ma'am" to me. Granted she was Southern and maybe five years younger than I was, but was I really looking that old? Not even twenty-seven yet!

Around that time R., the guy from the boat who had left his wife, hadn't given up on me, so I also threw him a bone by inviting him into my coterie of beaux. In the spirit of full disclosure, I cop to Bill Clinton's term "it" when asked how many men I'd gone to bed with. My answer is, "Only a few," with fingers crossed and the thought, Well, you didn't ask about couches, floors, elevators, or standing up.

My son calls me his Drama Mama.

And, truth be told, I admit I was playing Wronged Woman Goes to Hell to the hilt.

Meantime, the acting gig on the River Queen had ended. Hoping to end my moral spiral, I had an inspiration. What better time to stir up the pot even further and make a seismic shift in my life than by pursuing a fresh start somewhere else— at the same time possibly furthering my acting career by diving into a bigger pond! I'd leave New Orleans. I was ready to be the next Meryl Streep. I contacted an important Hollywood director whom I had met once in New Orleans and who had told me he cared for me more than he should, and I asked if he would make my entrée into pictures a little easier. He told me to come to California but that he couldn't promise anything. I knew another old beau, Marty, a dynamic and handsome movie producer (with one amputated leg), who was situated in New York, and on whom I also felt I could count for help. He too told me there were no guarantees but that he'd give it a try. I reluctantly called my mother to ask if I could come home with Gary for a few days until I could get some clarity on whether to go to California or New York, needing a decompression break to figure it out. In New York one had more of a shot of being a serious actor than in Hollywood, where one is just another pretty face.

A major drawback with New York was, aside from Marty, I knew only one other person there, and he was toxic, *non grata*, yesterday's news! I certainly didn't need to scratch at my barely healing heart scabs. It was a huge dilemma. Ever loving and nurturing, Mother's tight voice made sounds like "all right," but the subtext was similar to what she had previously told me when, penniless, I once asked in desperation for a small loan: "You made your bed, you lie in it." But this time, possibly reminded of her own situation when she had to return and live with *her* parents, it was hard to refuse me. So she granted a short visit while her impetuous daughter decided what to do with the rest of her misbegotten life.

I suppose I'm painting too flat a picture of my mother. Other people adored her. Needless to say, there were moments in my life when she was pleasant, even fun, but they were few and far between. Perhaps it was just our chemistry or I was too much like her. I'll never know. (The good thing she taught me was what *not* to be to my children.)

Upon making all the arrangements, closing my house, paying up bills, packing, and such, my friends delighted me with a big going-away party. Many of my co-actors, Playboy bunny friends, even ex-boyfriends came. For me it was a mixed bag of anticipation and profound sadness. I had lived in New Orleans for nine years. It had been full of beginnings and endings, failures, successes, and irony because, as Jack Shelton once so sardonically put it when the Desire Street streetcars were exchanged for buses bearing the same name, "See? Desire is a bus!" Now I was starting a new chapter, but this time as a single mother, again with no money (vengeful Al Fisher had not been generous and, retaliating for me opting out, agreed to the divorce with a mere $25.00 a month for child support), with no job in mind, and an almost three-year-old completely dependent on me. All I did have was a desperate person's faith and determination, trusting in my fairy tale ending.

We, Part One
DISTRESS AND DATSTRESS

DEPARTURE DAY IN NEW ORLEANS was cold and wet. Luckily I had decided on a train to Chicago, because the whole Eastern seacoast was blanketed with a record freeze, leaving many airlines with canceled flights. I had wisely booked a private compartment for Gary and me, anticipating a long, arduous trip. Al Belletto, with a sweet bouquet of flowers, took us to the station. He hugged Gary and told him to take care of Mommy because he was The Man now, and when we kissed goodbye it was with promises to keep in touch.

A few minutes after the train began to move from the station, I had barely settled in, trying to get Gary to nap, and putting things in order. Tears streamed down my face as I gazed out the window, the image of ice pelting the glass blending with my falling tears as I thought back on Al and my love affair.

I have what I consider a rather photographic recollection, at least of the early part of my life, a vivid visual sensory ability to remember minutia and details that have become the architecture of my memory scrapbook down to the smallest detail and, in particular, everything involved with meeting Al Markim. When I describe what I wore, said, did, I'm not drawing on poetic license. I'm as truthful as I know how. When I approached Jack Robinson in the kitchen as a four-year-old, I know that my pajamas had footies and little animals. When I say the grapes I offered Art Kramer were green, it's because I know they were. The sheets on my bed when Al Fisher tucked me in were lilac and had a slightly musty smell from the humid weather. And on my first night with Al Markim, I almost fainted from my intensely beating heart when he grabbed me and we fell to the floor as I scrambled out of my ivory dress (and ran to the bathroom to remove the push-up pads from my bra).

I've refrained from describing the phenomenal impact I felt making, and falling in, love with him because, as I said, I can't do it justice without it sounding trite. So it is with trepidation that I trustingly put this out here: what we called our Miracle on Catina Street.

It happened in the beginning of our affair, when we saw each other sporadically whenever he could get to the Crescent City. On one of those visits, we had come back to my place on Catina Street. The sitter had left. Gary was asleep. I fixed us a bite to eat, and we chilled for a while, basking in our newness, our possibilities. After a bit we went into my bedroom.

We were lying as in a cocoon, spoon-like on my bed, post-coital, with a single candle lighting the room. Then, *poof*, it went out. That can happen sometimes, I know, but after several moments, lying in the dark, he told me for the first time that he had fallen in love with me—and at that exact moment the candle burst again into flame.

I'm aware of how corny that sounds, but there it was. We were crazy in love, soul mates. He called me his Happiness Creature, and he was my Alfredo. I was so loved!

And now, sitting on that Chicago-bound train, I was never so not.

And then there was a knock on the compartment door.

Unbelievably, standing on the other side was R., holding a dozen red roses. "What in God's name are you doing here?" I asked, astounded. Wanting to surprise me, and knowing I'd be sad, he had booked a small lap on the train to take him for a few stops just to be with me a little longer! I don't recall much of that episode, just that I had never seen a grown man cry the way he did. (He continued to call me for years on end, until the unfed flame finally extinguished itself.) And he told me that the weather had so paralyzed the Northeast, and Chicago in particular, that all public transportation—buses, taxis, everything—were inoperative. Even private motorists were not chancing the icy streets. I wondered how I'd even get to my mother. I psyched myself with a pep talk that all would work out, reassuring myself that there were glimmers of my getting over the worst of Al's loss. It didn't help that he reneged on his promise and still kept in touch on the phone occasionally, so he knew I was leaving New Orleans. I told myself I was weaning myself from him, and that surely I'd find another love. Probably our end was the best thing that had happened to me!

When the train finally pulled into Chicago, I steeled myself to the fate awaiting me there, starting with my mother's attitudes and wondering how the hell we were going to get home. I gathered our things, along with the two bouquets of flowers, took Gary's hand, and prepared to disembark. All bundled up, we stepped down from the train into air so bitterly cold that for a second it felt hot—it slapped my face with a stinging frost enveloping any bare skin and forming minuscule icicles on my eyelashes, which, however, didn't prevent my eyes from seeing what I saw.

Standing next to a long, black limo stood the most incredible vision my world-weary eyes had ever beheld. In a black cashmere coat and white scarf, with a luminous smile that took over his whole face, and holding a bouquet of yellow roses, (the only relief against the otherwise stark gray/white of the day), stood Al Markim! Seeing him filled me to the brim. He swept toward us, smelling like winter and home, grabbed me in his arms—making me drop my bouquets—and kissed me, tasting like more, more, more, launching the true beginning of my life.

Perhaps what begs the question is why he didn't stick to his resolve, and why I too caved and went to New York. Although reuniting with Al was bliss, I guess I didn't want to read the tea leaves. I was back at square one, still at Nowhere, hadn't passed *Go*. He wasn't going to leave his family, and I wasn't going to be his mistress. My intention had been to clarify my next move by staying with my mother for a while.

But that fiasco of a week energized me more than ever to get airline tickets for Outta There and leave as fast as I could. Mother was clearly not happy being imposed upon. So, like, Bye, Felicia!

And Al kept calling me, begging me to come East. Recalibrating, I capitulated, decided to give the bad situation with Al another try. He might finally come to me permanently, I told myself, or I might fall out of love and find someone else.

I found a place on West Sixty-eighth Street near Central Park, put Gary in a nursery school, got a baby-sitter, found work as a part-time Kelly girl, and landed some very small jobs acting, such as in a bit part on the soap *As the World Turns* and some other minor commercial gigs Al found for me.

One such job was a commercial for a soap company. I was to stand near a washing machine over a dirty shirt and point my finger at the "ring around the collar." I found it incredible that three different men were futzing over my hand! First they had to put extra makeup on the veins, and then they didn't like the shadow my hand made on the shirt. It took *over an hour* just to get it right! This infuriated me. I'd been a big-deal actress, and here I was doing lowly stuff and expected to be grateful for the chance!

What I lived for were the stolen, incandescent moments we had together (so much for Al's credo "never in New York"). The only time I felt fully animated was with him. It was not the narrative I wanted, having to be duplicitous, "the other woman" sucking hind tit, as it were, frantically fitting in those hurried trysts as best we could, leaving me with anemic dribs and drabs, but that was the hand I had been dealt. The situation was worse being in the same city, having to endure the Other Woman's typical lonely Thanksgiving and Christmas (diner) dinners with my little boy while hearing Al delightedly recount the fun holidays with his family.

For many months I accepted this demeaning situation.

Then he made the move to be a movie producer. He began working with Jack Dreyfus of the Dreyfus Fund (with whom he had become friendly) on his movie *The Fool Killer*. He sent for me (and Gary—I'd never leave him with the sitter) to join him near the set in Knoxville, Tennessee. Cognizant of any noticeable untoward expenses at home that might send up a red flag to his wife, he put us up in a motel so cheap that scurrying roaches sent us scurrying away. But I had made my bargain with the devil and persevered.

Regarding my career on the Great White Way, I can't overstate my frustration. Big New-Orleans-*River Queen*-me was little New York pee drop. I was like Marjorie Morningstar after all! (If you've forgotten or never knew, she was a character in a book who endlessly strove to become a famous actress, to no avail.) Getting work was daunting. I'd go for interviews and, more often than not, come away with requests for my phone number but not my resume. To get work you had to be a member of Screen Actor's Guild; to be a member of SAG, you had to have an agent see your work; and an agent would not see you unless you were working in something!

So I kept my job as a Kelly Girl secretary to afford nursery school and pay for the baby-sitter. In the kitchenette of our tiny one-and-a-half-room apartment, there were cans of mac and cheese and, in the fridge, milk and gifted champagne. In those days it was all I could do to afford enough money for our basic needs (and my scotch and cigarettes). I don't think Al knew the extent of my dire financial situation, nor did I want him to, since I wouldn't accept anyone supporting me. I did date some men (free meals), however—Al was occasionally sleeping with his wife, so he could hardly object—but I kept my relationships platonic. So once again I was depending on dinners at fancy restaurants.

My poor child referred to Al and the men I dated as "Uncle Daddy." When Al Fisher was in town, he'd take Gary for a weekend, but that was sporadic. I tried to spend as much quality time with Gary as I could, even taking him with me on some dates. And there were some occasions of fun: to our delight, Al Markim would occasionally have time to play wrestling games with him on the floor, making a to-do, grunting and pretending to be defeated, and so on. Gary loved that. He needed a constant male in his life. I can't imagine what he thought seeing his mommy constantly kissed and being embraced in Al's arms, or going out with so many Uncle Daddies. Some of my dates would bring him great toys, and I remember a Ukrainian man I went out with who had a boat we'd go water-skiing on with Gary at the helm, and a sea plane he let us take the other wheel of for a bit. I also dated a very wealthy man (he owned Magnavox) whose fancy chauffeur-driven limo would come for me on one night and I'd be all dressed up in fancy clothes and heels, and then the next night a TV director I'd met while doing some acting on *As the World Turns* would pick me up on his motorcycle and I'd be in jeans and a helmet. I suppose nosy neighbors had stuff to talk about!

One night when the live-in Spanish baby-sitter had taken the night off, I was putting Gary to sleep. I had known his first words were *caballo*, for horse, and *avion*, for airplane, but I was rather surprised when, preparing to say his prayers that night, my little Jewish three-year-old crossed himself on his chest and began to recite, "En el nombre de el padre y la madre. . . ."

And regarding my little three-year-old, there are some moments in those difficult years that stick out as particularly excruciating. Desperately insecure and feeling more hopeless with each day of being a single mother with no money and no support, and getting nowhere with Al, I was unprepared when one day Gary asked me, "Mommy, what happens at the end of our days?" For some reason, that killed me, and I felt like I was going to break down. I couldn't think of the right reply to explain death...I couldn't give him a father, or even a mother who was stable and reassuring. I don't remember my reply—just his question that deserved some sort of answer, and that pains me to this day.

This "arrangement," a roller-coaster of pretense and deceit, living on the "down low," went on until July 29, 1963.

Then something shifted in me. Maybe it dawned on my lizard brain that I was getting older and nowhere and that, if I didn't call it quits, I was going to be left without a seat when the music stopped.

To my astonishment, however, when I read Al the same ultimatum terms as before, he agreed to leave his wife and said that, in fact, would tell her that very night.

It was around eight p.m. when he left my apartment. With my heart in my mouth and the pit of my stomach turning to acid, I waited. And waited.

As I have said, there have been three catastrophically dark times in my life, the first the sick miasma of my stepfather and adulterous mother. The debacle of my first marriage with Jack Shelton was no picnic. Leaving him and being alone on my own in a strange city was pretty brutal. I remember the words he spoke when I told him we were through—"It's a tragedy!" It was for me too, but I was unrelenting. Leaving Al Fisher was no picnic either, especially seeing his pain when he left Gary, but I knew the marriage was doomed, and that it was best to end it while Gary was still young enough not to be that affected. Those divorces were very sad but nothing like the apocalypse of that July 29 evening.

Over and over, I listened to Stan Getz's "Desafinado"—which I now can't abide. I was drinking way over my usual allotment of scotch on the rocks, and smoking pack after pack of cigarettes. I remember the dim golden cast of the lamp on my desk as I wrote a note to Al, which I planned to preemptively give him if and when he came back to me. It basically said I knew he couldn't do it and we were F-I-N-I-T-O.

Sometime around midnight, he showed up with red-rimmed eyes and without a smile or suitcase. He leaned against the wall, smoothing the hair on the top of his head, which, along with biting a cuticle, was a "tell" of his that signaled deep concentration or insecurity. Before he could say a word, I finessed him with the note. He looked pitiful as he explained how he had told Billie about us, and that she had made a terrible scene in front of the children, not sparing them, crying hysterically (I shudder thinking of the effect that had on them), begging him for one more chance, even telling him, "Keep Sondra as a mistress, but don't leave." He couldn't refuse her. Game over.

I didn't need to hear more. I insisted upon the same terms as before: I also told him very succinctly, "You've got to go back with the right attitude to make it work. You've got to find out if you need to leave her because the marriage isn't good, and not because of me." With an overwhelming hollowness, I closed the door, leaving sheer emptiness in his wake.

I swallowed what was left in a bottle of Valium, along with what was left in my bottle of Scotch. The rest is a total blur. All I remember was our friend Hesh being at my apartment—I've no recollection of calling him. He walked me around and around the place, plying me with cups of black coffee and finally putting me to bed and to blissful black.

As I said, I can only characterize the period from July 29 to the following October as a chasm, a black hole. My sense of self and security had the weight of meringue. It was so devastating a rupture that it rendered me incapable of turning to my default-fix methods: I was so turned off that I couldn't even look at another man.

Embarrassingly, I kept almost losing it. I'd walk around fighting tears. Once, on a bus to go to work, the driver had pudgy fingers that reminded me of Al's. A whiff of cigar smoke (Al had smoked cigarillos) would undo me completely. And any romantic music—bossa nova, sax, violin sounds, and I was mush.

Instead of resorting to triggering the usual chaos around me, however, it started to ease up a bit and, sometime around Halloween, to thaw. I spent more time with Gary, I kept busy working as a Kelly Girl, and I met a cool guy named Charlie Green who was much needed non-stop laughs and to whom I vomited my sad story. He became a Father Teresa to me, strictly a kindred soul who took me to the theater, to dinner, and to charade parties, my favorite thing. He had an aunt who worked as a clothes designer in motion pictures. Al was working then as an associate producer for a guy named Ely Landau, involved with a movie called *The Pawnbroker* that would earn an Academy Award for Rod Steiger and be Quincy Jones' first work in film. Charlie Green's aunt was working on the picture, too. I've no idea how Al learned of my relationship with Charlie, but one day Charlie brought me a note. It read: *Life has no meaning, all color is gone, nothing means anything without you, please could I contact you. Alfredo.*

Although the words were oxygen, I was resolute, determined to heal, and ignored the note.

THE NEXT MONTH, ON A CLEAR, crisp late November day, walking from the taxi that brought me home from my first real date—the first man I'd been intimate with since Al—I felt something resembling hope. This guy was extremely personable, good-looking, well off, and an authentic possibility of Life After Al. At home, after greeting my son, I had started fixing some breakfast when the doorbell rang.

And there he was: Al Markim, with a single yellow rose in one hand and a suitcase in the other.

FROM THAT DAY ON, WE DID NOT LOOK BACK. And he brought me yellow roses every week for years after. I would love and be faithful to him for more than half a century—fifty-three years of marriage to be precise.

That very weekend, on November 22, President Kennedy got killed. They not only lost their father but the father of their country. Furthermore, all was not so la-di-da happily ever after for me either, because one of the things Al asked before clinching our deal was that I give up all my aspirations for an acting career. I wasn't happy about it but felt his sacrifices exceeded mine, so I agreed. I would live to resent that promise, but, in hindsight, I think he was right. He knew my frailties and weaknesses. He often called me "Skitter" because I had such thin skin that the slightest perceived hurt would throw me into terrible doldrums, and he was familiar with the Harvey Weinsteins of this world. It is not inconceivable, had I taken that difficult acting road, I might not have been able to survive.

(YOU CAN'T STOP THE CREATIVE juices, though. Like a river, blocked, the water will find a way to trickle down by other means. Two years into out marriage, I wrote a novel, *The Yearning*, sitting in our hot attic and typing on an old-fashioned typewriter. But, just as had happened the time I didn't accept the great opportunity to use the scholarship from the Chicago Art Institute, I blew a chance at getting the book published. When I finished writing it, I was able miraculously to get it seen by Sam Vaughan, the president of Doubleday, who made some suggestions, but all I could see was that he had rejected my perfect prose. . .so I put the book away in a drawer. Idiot! My girlfriend Sarah used to tell me I had a fear of success and often sabotaged myself. Some years later, Debby Reynolds told me the same thing. Al was working with her on a videotape called *Do it Debby's Way,* and we were at dinner one evening when I mentioned a book of essays I was working on at the time, *Rhinestones of Wisdom*. She offered to look at it and perhaps help me with her connections, but I never sent it to her.)

At that time, I had started a career as a lyricist. I was writing with some talented musicians like Bobby Scott, who wrote "A Taste of Honey," as well as Quincy Jones (with whom we would become friendly, having him over for dinner and such—Al would get him to Landau and his first shot at working in motion pictures on *The*

Pawnbroker). I also cut a record with Miriam Makeba ("Same Moon In Sky Over Me"), among others. I enjoyed a small measure of success until I eventually got a check from ASCAP for twelve cents (and once, actually, for $000.00!). In another way we would later make money, I also dubbed motion pictures for a man named Jack Tropp. I'd have a projector, interpretive script, and paper and pencil, watch a foreign film, and write down English words to fit into the actors' mouths. I'd even write dubbed songs, no easy feat. (I liked the challenge, but when the going got tough I skipped off to test a different talent—not a paradigm conducive to success!)

But after Al came to me with his suitcase, we moved to an apartment building on Riverside Drive, in a tony neighborhood on the West Side, a few blocks from his kids. Al took a studio apartment on the second floor a few floors under mine. We got a second phone for him to use in my apartment, since that's where he was most of the time. Al's divorce wasn't final yet, and since we had to be discreet, I kept it under my bed, so if anyone called him, he could answer, pretending he was at his own place.

Al Fisher had visitation rights, and he'd frequently come get Gary, who was then four and a half. One day, I was in bed with a cold when he arrived. He had a friend's dog with him as he popped in to say hi.

At that moment the phone under my bed started ringing. He looked around and asked, wasn't I going to get it? I told him it wasn't my phone. But since it kept ringing unanswered, he asked, "Well, what *is* that?"

"What's what?" I punted, faking a cough to muffle the sound. Finally, I told him it was the neighbors' phone; we had really thin walls! He seemed dumbfounded but let it go. The dog kept nosing under the bed. Thank goodness Gary grabbed him, and the dog started licking his face. I told Gary to go wash his face, which he obediently did. When he came back from the bathroom, he asked, "*Now* can I kiss the doggie?"

Al's little sublet had a single piece of furniture—a cot to sleep in (when he wasn't sneaking up to my place to sleep with me and then getting up very early, before Gary did, going to the service elevator, shoes in hand, and sneaking back to his sublet). He had not even a chair or table, just that cot, for he wasn't planning to be there long. As soon as the divorce papers came through, it would be *adios* sublet.

One night we had been in his studio apartment for some reason and, being young and in love, got carried away and found ourselves on that tiny cot. I was squished half on top of him, resting, and relishing the afterglow. Al, as he often did after lovemaking, fell into a deep sleep. He started to snore and I thought, Oh, how sweet, how precious, his snoring! Anyone who knows me will get the irony in that. For a good half of our married life, because of his snoring and my acute and hypervigilant hearing, we didn't sleep in the same bed. We'd be together till the last moment, but when it was time to drift off, I departed for another bedroom. But in those early days, when we couldn't get enough of each other, we were glue.

At age 3, getting a new dress for reciting the Four Questions on Passover

At 22, in New Orleans

Al in the Space Cadets *TV series at 25*

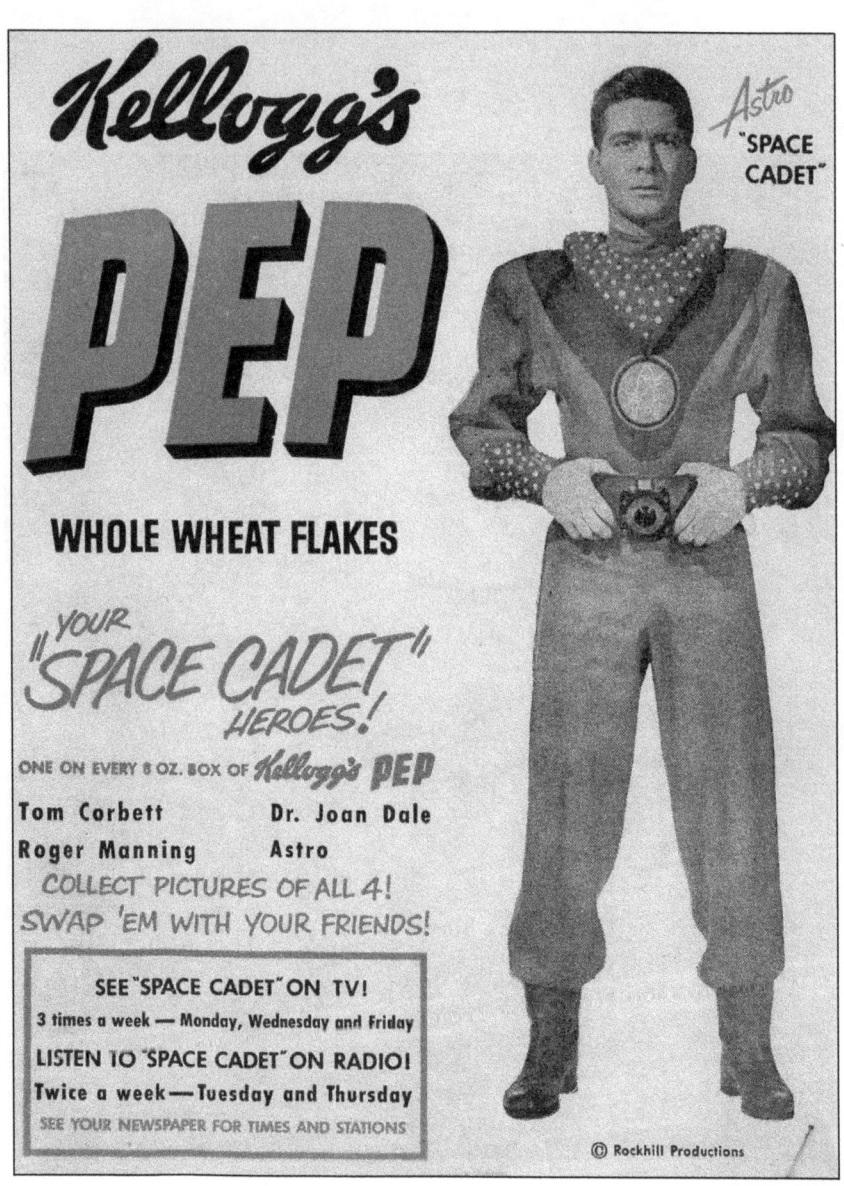

Al on a Kellogg's cereal box, age 26

Al on the cover of TV Guide, *age 27*

A signature look at age 25

Al when I first met him in 1961

Aboard the River Queen

In New York at 26

With Al in 2007

Performing Love Letters *together, 2011*

At Nick's bar mitzvah, 2014. Standing, from left, John, Ryan, Matt, Julie, Fred, Nancy, Carla, Gregg, Gary, Dan, Avery, and Jeff. Seated, Nina, Becky, Jessica, me, Al, Nikki, Sue, and Jordan. In front, Nick, Brian, and Josh

At Nancy and Gary's wedding, 2015: from left, Josh, Fred, Nikki, Carla, Nancy Jessica, Sue, Becky, John, Dan, me, Matt, Ryan, Nina, Avery, Jeff, Jordan, Julie, and Nick. In front, Gary, Nancy, and Brian

Toward the end (photograph courtesy of Julie Birks)

We, Part Two

THERE'S AN ICEBREAKER PARTY GAME in which you list three surprising truths about yourself plus a lie, and someone guesses the lie. Here's my list:

1. *I was the only white woman at a Voodoo in Haiti.*
2. *I danced with the Shah of Iran at the El Morocco nightclub.*
3. *I had dinner with Mickey Mantle.*
4. *I got married six times.*

In this case, they're all true. The Voodoo moment occurred with Jacques de la Verne, on our trip. The second happened when I was on a date, and an aide of the Shah asked his permission for a dance with me. We did the Charleston! Another date was a friend of Mantle's; there were others there, but it didn't stop him from making a drunken move on me!

The fourth needs a bit more explanation. The first time Al and

I married was the Christmas Eve before our designated official wedding, on January 10. We needed the five-hundred-dollar tax deduction, so, along with Al's parents, we scrambled to Newark, New Jersey—where my divorce had come through—taking the Tubes to get there. It was Christmas Eve, and City Hall was full of raucous, drunk, and celebrating people, including the judge. He made us swear to be "*Fidel*," and that was it.

The second time Al and I married, the official one, was held in a rabbi's study in Manhattan with family and friends; even our children attended—Al's eldest, Nancy, age ten; Danny, age seven; my Gary, five; and Al's Nina, four.

The third time was in Bucks County, Pennsylvania, at a candy store on Windy Bush Road, where the proprietor—doing double duty as a justice of peace—was interrupted a couple of times by a bell to take care of a customer, while Al, rather inelegantly dressed in jeans, was chewing gum, and I, equally casual, chomped away on red licorice. We wanted to get married there because Bucks County had been a place we often visited to shack up. One of those times, in passing the Windy Bush candy store with the *Justice of the Peace* sign, we promised we'd marry there for the kicks. Truthfully, I think after all we'd been through, we just wanted to be certain our marriage was impenetrable.

The fourth time came as a surprise. Al was a hopeless romantic. For example, on our eleventh anniversary he placed an ad on the bottom of the *New York Times* front page that read *Happy Anniversary, Sondra. You're the best thing that ever happened to me.* This time, unbeknownst to me, he got it in his head to surprise me by retaking our vows, the subterfuge being we were going to the theater. In the car, he told me he had to make a quick business stop and parked in front of the same rabbi's study where we'd officially gotten married. I didn't make any connection and was settling in to wait in the car when he asked me to accompany him. I trudged up the stairs to the study—and into an avalanche of our friends and our kids shouting, "Surprise!"

When the judge asked if I did, I almost said, "No," because I hadn't dressed in a cute enough outfit or had my hair done.

(Another side note: Years later, when my sister Vivien got engaged and asked me to be her bridesmaid, I quipped, "Always a bride, never a bridesmaid!")

IN OUR FIRST MONTHS TOGETHER, I had finally realized my dream and was supremely happy. Luckily, being a lyricist at the time, and since New York City gave allowances to professionals, we were able to obtain a fabulous rent-controlled apartment on Seventy-ninth and Riverside Drive, three short blocks from where Al's children lived on Eighty-second, a prerequisite for him.

Sweetest of all, a little over a year later, I became pregnant with our daughter Carla. From the moment she was born, she was a gift of pure sunshine, even foregoing the two o'clock feeding. My first-born had been all dark-haired and -eyed, and my second all blonde and light-eyed, so I had my Ken and Barbie —and when you threw in the other three delightful children, I felt my cup had run over, notwithstanding the great adjustments to be made.

Stepmother-hood was no easy task. But with the same passion I applied to anything I felt important, I threw myself into being Stepmother of the Year, and perhaps overdid it. I was trying too hard to win them over and not making much headway until I took some good advice from our friend Jane, who told me not to hover over them the way I did. "Leave them alone, and they'll come home wagging their tails." But I had so desperately wanted it to work, sometimes to the detriment of slighting Gary (so they would not be jealous of him living with their father), giving him anemic attention compared to what I lavished on them.

We were keenly aware of how the children struggled with mixed allegiance to their parents, and how they picked up subtle nuances of hostility. It was a difficult disconnect for them, and a struggle for all of us.

But it was such a high for me having the man I loved as my husband that I didn't mind devoting myself to them, wiping their noses, mending their cuts, kissing their boo-boos, feeding and nursing them if they got sick on our watch, and tucking them into bed at night with my special lullaby, "Lu-lu-lu Lullabye," while I stroked their foreheads and asked them to tell me the best and worst thing that had happened that day. It was a sneaky way for us to try incorporating our values, telling them our best and worse as well, showing them adults were vulnerable too, and discussing how to deal with the bad stuff but ending on a happy note. I also made up a Bad Dream Spray by removing the label on a nice-smelling room spray and writing *Bad Dream Spray* on it. I would use it when needed, and it mostly worked! (If you're a young person reading this, tuck these tricks into your memory for the future.) Also, I created all sorts of fun games, including scavenger hunts—in rhyme, no less—that they adored. The saving grace was that Al's children were wonderful. Adorable and intelligent, they had exemplary manners and were easy to love. I was glad for Gary to have siblings and now be part of a family. I was challenged to win the children over, determined to make the blended marriage blend, but it was like banging my head against steel. Billie, unsurprisingly filled with rancor, did everything she could to disrupt the transition. In those days, divorce laws favored the mother. One couldn't fault Billie for fighting back, knowing Al was over a barrel and would do anything to get as much visitation as possible, and he paid dearly for it. The High Cost of Leaving left us with barely enough money to feed ourselves. Sixty percent of our income went in alimony. My weekly food allowance was twenty-five dollars. Granted it was in the early Sixties, but the takeaway for me was real deprivation. I relied on the kindness of strangers—my girlfriend Joy gave me her hand-me-down clothes, and other friends their spare furniture. I worked nights for a legal secretary, getting paid under the table, and did more dubbing; Al worked with Landau but also on the side with Jack Dreyfus on another picture. Rather than buy new shirts, we turned Al's frayed shirt collars, and he brought a brown bag with cottage cheese to work for lunch. I painted everything—pictures, walls, the ugly exposed pipes in the bathroom—instead of buying art or decorative adornments. We eked and eked. Not to belabor the point, though ecstatic as his wife, I found the ramifications beyond formidable. Al used to say, "One of the true marks of maturity is the ability to handle ambivalence." I tried. I made valiant efforts, telling myself to suck it up, but apparently I was not yet mature enough. With the aid of my go-to medicine—Scotch—I took my frustration out on Gary. Having been thrust into big-time coping changes, not the least of which, was losing his Number One Man status, he was becoming very difficult. Lashing out in just the way I'd been programmed to by reliving my mother's form of relief from frustration, at times I began taking to beating Gary. My method, using a shoe or a hairbrush on his butt, was at least not as bad as what my mother used on me: a fly swatter, a mop, a belt, her fists—until Al insisted I ease up on the throttle and put a stop to it. Still, I was unforgivably abusive, something I'll always regret.

We are the victims of victims, and pain not transformed is transmitted.

HOWEVER, NOTHING IS FOREVER. . .neither happiness nor misery. In time, Al's career grew successful enough for money to finally become less of a hardship. My *modus vivendi*—to make our family work—finally started to be realized. We found our niche. It evolved a social life highlighted by a weekly poker game with terrific friends, which became integral to our lives. Our kids today still talk of falling asleep to laughter and the tinkle of poker chips. Nothing interfered with our game. When Al and I had baby Carla, we brought her with us and laid her down to sleep either in an open bureau drawer or between coats on the host's bed. Hesh, one of our friends, had a stepson whose bar mitzvah occurred on our hallowed poker night. (Imagine!) As soon as the bar mitzvah was over, we all rushed from the temple to their place in the village for drinks, dinner, and our game.

Dinner was shrimp. One must have been tainted, because while we were playing, I started getting warm and itchy. Everyone told me, "Shut up and deal," but it got so bad that, hoping to alleviate it, I went to the bathroom, got undressed, filled the tub and got in. When my throat started to close, they finally got the message. Al and another friend, Herbie, took me to nearby St. Vincent's Hospital, where they gave me a shot of Benadryl. Instead of taking me home, however, they went right back to the game. I actually sat there, trying to keep my eyes open, unable to make out the cards because of the spots in them, but I continued trying, knowing the show had to go on. And it did, for years—until Herbie got caught cheating on his beautiful wife Sarah, and that was the end of our beloved poker games. We never forgave him!

Taking out a loan, we moved to our first house—a little sugar-maple split in the leafy suburb of Closter, and soon after put in a pool. Since the house was on a cul-de-sac with wall-to-wall neighborhood kids, our own became quite popular.

The Monday after we had the pool installed, a beautiful day, the kids off to school, Al off to work, was a seminal day because I remember getting into the water and feeling so grateful and pleased that my life had finally given me what I wanted. It couldn't have been more than just a few minutes later when it hit me: Now what? I was alone in my new house in a new neighborhood, I had nothing creative to do, I had "made it," but now what? The Peggy Lee song, "Is That All There Is" surfaced for a few minutes, but I quickly dismissed it and splashed around til the feeling left and I started planning the dinner menu.

Peggy Lee resurfaced later that day as I put the laundry in the washer. I was annoyed that Gary's shirt was hopelessly stained, and it hit me again. The shirt seemed emblematic, somehow reminding me of the old fairytale of the lady who lived in a vinegar bottle. She was happy that way till her fisherman husband came home one day and told her how he'd caught a magic fish that was willing to grant him any wish, but that he'd let the fish go.

    She was furious with him and ordered him to go back and find it and tell it to grant them a house, so she could get out of the vinegar bottle. (I'm condensing.) He does, it does, and the wife is happy in her new house. But after a while she tires of it and tells her husband to go back to the fish and get her a larger, better house. He does. She's happy. . .and then orders him to go back and get her a palace—she wants to be a queen, et cetera. Eventually, she sends him back and tells him she wants to be God, and the next scene finds her back in the vinegar bottle.

    Cleaning the stained shirt, I chided myself for being ungrateful. La-la-la, life is great. Be positive!

GARY'S FIRST CAR ALMOST GAVE Al a heart attack, though. Coming home from work one evening, he saw an ambulance parked in front of our house. He jumped out of the car and ran half-cocked into the house only to learn the vehicle was Gary's new wheels—the perfect vehicle for making out in the back, though he'd had to remove the red light on top.

    Gary also flourished in Closter because he could practice his budding talent for building. (In first grade, when he was asked what he wanted to be when he grew up, he had written *BLDR.*) At around twelve, with the help of some buddies, he built an elaborate tree house complete with an "elevator" made out of an intricate combination of ropes and wood. His biggest achievement was a one-room clubhouse for him and his friends; he even poured cement for its foundation. Our property was located near a brook that ran through our backyard. The phenomenal thing is how that shack withstood the flooding waters springing from the brook. Periodically, they got so bad they took down small trees and anything in their way, but not the shack.

I was so proud of him—until one particular afternoon. I prided myself on being ultra hip, having been around the block a few times and knowing the score, but I got totally freaked out by a real eye-opener. Al and I had been strolling around our yard when he noticed something untoward in the earth near our house that turned out to be the small exposed part of an electrical cord that seemed to be running underground from our place to somewhere else. The somewhere else was Gary's shack. "So *that's* why our electric bills are higher," Al muttered, and managed to unlock the shack door. I beheld a room the walls of which were covered with Mylar, surrounded by several powerful lamps lighting what appeared to be a garden of sorts. My first reaction was delight: "Al, look how clever! A garden!"

Al started pulling out the plants. "Sondra, it's *marijuana!*"

We thought the punishment we doled out would dissuade Gary from ever doing such a thing again, only to discover months later that he had not only returned to his horticulture ways, but that Nina was now in cahoots, and that they had enlisted six-year-old angel Carla to aid and abet, paying her pennies to water the plants, now hidden under the stairs in the basement!

Those were trying times. We kept disciplining but they kept trying!

Since Al was a pioneer in the video business, we had an opportunity to endear our neighbors to us. He brought home a video camera, virtually unheard of at the time, and "filmed" some of the kids playing football in the yard. We then invited their parents to come over for a drink, telling them we wanted to show them something on television. They had no idea they would soon see an instant replay of the event, and were blown away.

Another time Al brought home a videotape of the hit porn picture *Deep Throat*. Al's parents were visiting us at the time. Papa Julius—Al's dad—was a very sweet soul who could marvel at a leaf forever. An intelligent man but financially unsuccessful, he should have been a poet or a rabbi, because he wasn't cut out for business. We had to supplement their income (as well as my mother's farther down the road). Julius was also quite square and old-fashioned. A few years into our marriage, Billie, whose interactions with us were usually disagreeable and who was involved in some local charitable work, astonished us by asking if I'd do a small modeling bit to help her cause. I had a good friend named Johnny who was gay and loved doing my hair and makeup. He prepared me for the show and was in the audience, along with Al, Nana, and Papa. After the show, walking down the street for a block or two, Johnny and I, with our arms around each other's waist, ambled along dishing about the event, including praising Billie for being pleasant. Back in our apartment, Papa threw a fit! I'd never seen him like that—and never would again. Furious, he couldn't believe how disrespectful I had been embracing another man, and in front of my own husband! Al and I tried to calm him down, explaining that Johnny was gay. But there was no assuaging him. "How can you say that he isn't a man!" he spewed. "He was wearing *pants!*" But that was the only time I ever saw him raise his voice in such consternation.

I actually considered Papa one of the most successful men I'd ever known, lack of money notwithstanding. His marriage, his relationship with his family and friends, were beyond exemplary. As for Nana, a cute little Kewpie doll with a big smile on her face that made her look perpetually surprised, she was far from dumb but more naive than anybody I ever met, not the sharpest knife in the drawer; but she was, more importantly, a wonderful grandmother to the kids (who adored her tollhouse cookies), and she always tried being pleasant with me, albeit to the point of inanity.

I'll never forget one conversation between us that went right over her head. We had all been sitting around the dinner table, and, somehow, we got onto the subject of pet names for vaginas, vehemently defending our preferences. Nancy insisted it was "Tweeny," and I thought "Pootie" was better.

"But it's in between!" she said. "So it's Tweeny."

"No. The Peety is the boy, and the Pootie is the girl."

Nana and Papa had been observing this exchange with him looking aghast, though her perplexed expression seemed more incredulous. But she just kept smiling her big sunny, simple smile, finally finding her comfort zone, a giggle, and conferring her blessing on us: "God love 'em! Aren't they funny!"

(Along those lines, a girlfriend tells me how she used to place her three-year-old daughter on the potty to pee and, each time she did, point there and say, "That's a good girl!"

After a year or so, the daughter asked her, "What's my good girl really called?")

On the evening Al's parents were visiting us and he brought home *Deep Throat*, he asked if they wanted to see it. First their eyes silently communed, and apparently got the green light. Al put them in our bedroom where the VCR was, began the tape, and left them, closing the door behind. It took ten minutes for Nana to come running out of the room, her face red and without her ubiquitous smile. Her review consisted of one word: *"Feh!"* Papa didn't care for the picture either, but he stayed to watch the entire thing to be absolutely certain!

Gary and some buddies formed a band, and they rehearsed in our basement. Thankfully, we had cool neighbors, because their thunderous Led Zepellin renditions rocked the whole neighborhood so fiercely, I thought all our houses would be shaken off their foundations. But, stoic and tolerant, as passionately as I had once thrown myself into self-destruction, I did a total U-turn, cleaning up my act, and threw myself into being Wife and Mother of the Year.

My supreme hope was to avoid leaving our kids the legacy I'd been dealt, that the wake my parents had left me in would not be theirs. I became a gourmet cook, baked cakes (which, though tasty, came out lopsided because, impatient and clueless at math, I had trouble following baking recipes, so I struggled over instructions like "cream the butter." How much cream? I wondered.) I was class mother, Brownie leader, and embraced the children's activities to the extent that Carla's friends called me "Mrs. Mommy." I was also asked by my children's teachers (and later, my grandchildren's) to occasionally teach art, such a *papier mâché,* to them. My friend Sarah once drove all the way to Woodcliff Lake from where she lived an hour away to convey me to Montclair College to teach a class on *papier mâché* as well (and then drive me all the way back, since I hated driving at night). Somehow I also managed to open a little store where I created and sold little *papier mâché* figures. I named it Sondra's Serendipity, but it didn't do well, perhaps because nobody knew it was there—hence the cheap rent!

One of the achievements that I'm proudest of was what came to be known as "The Mary Stories." I'd tell tales, about a mischievous child who kept getting into trouble, that the children ate up. At the request of their mothers, I made tapes of my Mary stories (which even my nieces and nephews wanted), and they played them over and over.

As for "Perfect Wife," I insinuated myself into Al's world as much as possible, too. He loved my joining him on business dinners, if for no other reason than to complement his staid personality with my more audacious one, because, truth be told, Al could be let's say recalcitrant. For one thing, like most men I'd known, I had to pull deep emotions out of him with electric pliers. And though our sexual intimacy was deeply gratifying, even there I had to loosen him up. Sex is *fun*, ya know? No question that he loved it, his appetite hard to match, but sometimes even in that he could be a bit *serious*. When we went out to business dinners, there is no question that Al pushed me off on clients to charm, like a dog: "Go sic 'em!" And I had the hubris to do so. I was an "asset" (to music?). At Teletronics, I often subbed as personnel director, and did some on-camera promos and whatever else I could. We had a date night every Wednesday, so I'd get to his office a couple hours early and schmooze with the employees, keeping in the management's vein of welcoming "hominess," and also because I truly liked them.

It was an extraordinary place with wonderful people, many of whom, even today decades later, still have Teletronics party reunions and participate in a Teletronics Facebook Group.

Much of that time, I was floating in a bubble of contentment. And it was a kick rubbing elbows with the occasional celebrity (I have in my kitchen what I call my ego wall: various pictures of us, with people like Frank Sinatra and Ted Kennedy, and one of Dan Quail looking down at my cleavage). Date night was a highlight—and included fun evenings at places like Studio 54 and eating at the best restaurants (on the company dime)—but, in the interest of accuracy and not putting too fine a point on our happy life then, much was also humdrum, and I readily confess there was just so much I could take of the suburbs and dealing with the predominant themes: cookies, curtains, and kids. (I much preferred peppering conversations with questions like, "What do you think is the biggest misconception about yourself?" or "Name one thing you like about yourself and one thing you don't," or "What do you know today you didn't yesterday?" or "Tell me a secret!" That's just how I roll.)

But though I may not have known it then, I see, in retrospect, that, Peggy Lee or not, it was a terrific place to bring up our kids, and I wouldn't trade that time for anything. Sometimes "ordinary" is not a bad thing. Ask anyone in a hospital bed.

We: Part Three

WHEN NINA WAS ABOUT FIFTEEN, she came to live with us. The precipitating circumstance, I thought, was her falling in love with a boy named Joey Pecarraro. Nina wanted to extend her visitation, so she could spend more time with him. But according to her, it wasn't because of Joey, but because life at home had become untenable; she didn't want to live and fight anymore with her mother, who had given her an ultimatum: If she stayed with us longer than the allotted visitation, she shouldn't come home at all.

But since I wasn't there, I don't know for sure. All I know is, neither Al nor I ever *asked* Nina to stay with us. We also never badmouthed Billie, though I wanted to, having heard she often dissed us. I had to be careful not to alienate the children, and Al insisted we take the high road, so my not-too-tasty diet consisted of swallowing resentments. In addition, the children had to be careful not to trigger anger in their mother, to the extent that they'd hide anything endearing I might have taught them. They would tell Billie, "Dulcie taught us this cute game," meaning a friend of theirs, rather than say "Sonj," their name for me.

Having Nina live with us was an immense bonus that added to my blessings. All three children had their ambivalence cut out for them. Danny, torn by allegiances to both parents, liked coming to the suburbs because, aside from adoring his dad, there were baseball games he could play in, but the rest of it was particularly difficult on him. Nancy, the oldest, wisely sought some therapy but, more importantly, was into her own life as well as a boyfriend who took up most of it, so she handled it better, at least ostensibly.

Of course the divorce was exceedingly difficult for the children. It killed Al and me to see their pain. The struggle and adjustment varied from child to child. It's illustrative to point out how they reacted upon learning it was happening. Billie insisted Al tell them by himself that their lives were about to be phenomenally upended. So he sat them down and broke it to them.

Nancy, who was about twelve, immediately got up to fix hot chocolate for everyone, and Danny, three years younger, not wanting to hear another word, hid behind the drapes. A bit over five, Nina was oblivious. A couple of years later, when Al and I had been married long enough for me to be pregnant with Carla, she suddenly asked, "Daddy, when are you coming home?"

As for me, filtering through that "adjustment period" came sheer joy for finally achieving my dream and marrying Mr. Right.

During the Seventies I struggled, not only with those adjustments, but also with feeling thwarted big time by not acting any more. I thought I was supposed to have a life, too.

One day in particular, I had just gone to the A&P annoyed at having such restrictions on our pathetically limited budget. I felt overburdened, overweight, unattractive, and invisible—just another face in the crowd. It was almost three o'clock, time to pick up Carla from school.

As I was driving my seven-year-old home, she—always so in tune with my moods constantly soaking up any of my anxiety no matter how I tried faking—might have sensed my sadness and asked if I was okay. On a whim I decided to level with her. "You know, Carla, I used to be an actress, and people would applaud and like seeing me, but nowadays I'm just feeling very unimportant."

Pondering for a moment, she perked up, her face brightening and her cheerful voice proudly offering a solution. "Mommy! You should go back and be an actress!" Pause. "Just be home by three!"

In retrospect, most of those years in the Seventies were pretty terrific. The other day I heard Carol King's "I Feel The Earth Move" on my car radio and was immediately transported. With unabashed nostalgia, I was reminded of the countless barbecues, the pool, holiday, and birthday parties, their various sports activities, Carla's cheerleading, Gary's band gigs, transporting Nina and Carla to gymnastics, Gary to Hebrew school, the boys' sports activities, friends' houses, clothes shopping, you name it. I can visualize the willow trees in our front lawn, and, in the back, the pool, brook, and shack. I see our little Yorkie, Brandy, eternally sitting at the window, waiting for us to come home from wherever. I feel a sense of pride that we somehow managed to bring up our family emotionally and physically intact. The children all marched to their own drummers, true to their selves. And it is not without some small measure of wistfulness that I say this, because teaching them to think for themselves often backfired on us as parents. I dare to claim that the biggest achievement of my entire life is that this family blended with genuine love among them. We had no respite, for we would have to continue applying the same effort as each child grew up and married—in most cases, out of the Jewish religion—so that we had further personalities, and religions, to integrate. So we do a lot of celebrating, Chanukah, Christmas, because we were and are a family who enjoys hardy par-tays!

AS TO RELIGIOUS ADJUSTMENTS: When Nina's children were young, her Christian husband Mark would take them to church on Sundays. One day we were celebrating our big traditional *seder* (have you ever seen grown-up people choke on their drinks and sputter them all over themselves?) and about to make the blessing over the wine. It goes without saying that all of our children are geniuses, including little Ryan with his saucer-sized blue eyes and adorable personality. When Papa Al asked who could say the prayer in Hebrew, Ryan's hand shot up. He could barely lift the glass with both hands, but he managed in clear and perfect Hebrew to say, "*Baruch atah adonoi, aloheinu melech haolam, boray pri hagof-*

fen, in the name of Jesus, amen!"

Gary was flourishing with his band, which was great, and often, when they were playing, Al and I went to the gig. Some of those teenagers were rather cute, and I'd find myself caught between wanting to pat their eight-pack abdomens and straighten their messy hair! Like the villainess in my melodrama, I too was redeemed, a true and faithful wife—*but I wasn't dead!*

This Goody-Two-Shoes incarnation went just so far. On rare occasion I even shared a joint with the older Gary and his posse, but our children, each of them, turned out to be highly functioning, successful, well-integrated people who have not succumbed to addictions, so we must have done something right.

As for my newly turned leaf in the Faithful department, flirting seemed to be stuck in my DNA. (If I couldn't get attention on the stage anymore, fill in the blanks.) Truly, I might have been better suited to life on the Left Bank of Paris than in the conservative suburbs. But if I had any serious thoughts of dallying or returning to my old ways (with one serious exception that I'll explain later), I was quickly disabused of them at a party we went to.

As I've said, I wasn't dead just because I was married, and I'm sure that could be said for Al. He also liked a bit of flirting or, as he put it, being "charming," but nothing *serious*. I once asked him, "You cheated on Billie—why not me?"

"The difference is," he said, "I'm in love with you."

But then there was this party one Saturday night.

There are three types of men who have always gotten to me: Italians, musicians, and psychiatrists, dark-haired ones preferred. I don't know why, but there you have it! That night, invited to a *chichi* party in a swank penthouse in the city, one of the guests who caught my eye was a handsome Italian psychiatrist with thick black hair and long eyelashes. Someone poured too much wine down my throat, and that someone started to flirt with the shrink, and I was at that point of inebriation when I thought everything I said was witty and flawless, and, with little encouragement, I would have gotten up to dance a wild fandango—especially since Al, the rat, seemed to be deeply engrossed in conversation with a beautiful Asian woman!

Sometime during the evening, this psychiatrist suggested we, our spouses included, get together after the party for a *digestif* or some coffee. I eagerly seconded the motion, and we did.

Sipping coffee in a neighborhood café, the four of us chatting amiably, the doctor guy surreptitiously handed me a note under the table. I read the message the moment I was alone: *Let's have a scene soon. I'll call tomorrow.* My phone number? I'd *given* it to him? And had I agreed to a foursome? What had I gotten my flirty self into?

At that time we had a wonderful live-in housekeeper named Matilda. She was from the Dominican Republic and could hardly speak English, never a problem for me because I spoke Spanish. She sometimes answered our phone by saying, "Mahkey ho" ("Markim Home"). She had Sundays off. That night, lying in bed and unable to sleep, I stewed and fretted over how I was going extricate myself from the hot water I'd gotten into. I devised a plan: The next day, I'd be sure to answer the phone, and when he called, pretend (actress that I still was) that I was Matilda and tell him we weren't "Ho." Then, if he called the next day, a Monday when Al was at work, I could talk freely and provide regrets, mea culpas, and an *adios*. I sweated it out for most of the day; when the phone finally rang, I quickly picked it up in a room away from everyone and said, "Mahkey ho."

There was a long pause and then I heard a highly indignant Matilda say, "Mrs. *Mahkey?*"

I quickly retrieved those two goody shoes, he never called, and I stuck thereafter to ladies at parties and talked about curtains, cooking, and kids.

Living well is the best revenge. I was determined to make the family what my nuclear family hadn't been: close-knit, loving, and happy. I didn't do it alone.

Nancy married Fred Birks and had their first daughter, Jessica, followed by Julie. (It was about then that I established as a family tradition the annual family reunion, which still continues twenty-seven years later). Then Nina married Mark McCullough and had Becky, Ryan, and Matt. The marriage didn't last, but, as if *bashert* (that Yiddish term for something meant to be), it led her to John Laul, the absolutely right guy for her. Dan married Sue Slaven, and they begat Jeff, Nikki, and Jordan. It took Carla, very much into her career as a lawyer, a while to have her children, but her marriage to Gregg Siegel produced Josh, Nick, and Brian. Gary took his time but married Nancy Squires (before I died, Lord be praised!). As of this writing, the cherry on our cake is my grandson Jeff having married Avery Shelton, who gave birth to a son, Cash, so I now have a great-grandson, bringing our clan to twenty-four! Add the children from former marriages, do the math and, at a minimum, I'm sure I've added greatly to Hallmark Greeting Cards' business and subtracted from our bank account. (They also all have dogs, with the understanding that I love them too whether I want to or not.)

You give your children roots and wings.

We must have screwed up somewhere because all but one adopted the wings part. Dan lives in Austin, Texas; Gary in Ventura, California; Carla in Maryland; and Nina in Pennsylvania. Our token reasonably accessible kid is Nancy, who thoughtfully lives in Oakland, New Jersey, a forty-five-or-so-minute drive away, unless it's me driving, and then it's a half hour.

Whereas I once considered my stepchildren a formidable challenge, I've grown to love them dearly and can't imagine life without them. Al was a magnificent husband, and we were crazy in love. He called me his Happiness Creature. Our kids made fun of us because we were constantly holding hands and leaving love notes scattered everywhere. He'd call from work several times a day; I accompanied him on every business trip. Joined at the hip was our norm, and I know how it sounds. One may gag, but I loved it totally and still pine for that tender connection.

But have you ever wondered why stories end at *happily ever after*? The unexpected drama pretty much recedes, and the mundane, prosaic Everyday, with its grocery shopping, brushing teeth, emptying the dishwasher, going to the movies, burping and slurping, takes center stage. So I won't bore you with the years that comprised much of our marriage, for, again, they were mostly content and thus relatively unremarkable—not material for intriguing reading. However, lest we sit back smiling, thinking Little Sondra

SINGING LIGHT

Happy At Last, let me add that the pervasive disorder of my early life had left an indelible mark on me. Bursts of temper at times overtook me. I could be hateful, full of anger at Al and, not a psychiatrist, I can't explain why. I'd get exasperated at something—Al could be self-involved and confident nearly to the point of smugness at times—and I'd lose control. But they were short-lived outbursts, often forgotten with the help of voracious sex.

I know I detested not being "in the world" and was jealous that he was. That notwithstanding, our marriage was for lack of a better word, a happy one, and we were certainly blessed with terrific kids.

I've resisted the urge to heap excess praise on my progeny. Still, self-aggrandizement is hard to avoid in a memoir. I strive to but apologize if some leaks out.

Bragging about children and so forth reminds me of a note I once saw posted on a bulletin board in a swanky spa: *Don't tell me about how great your kids are; mine are great, too. Don't brag about how many fabulous trips you've been on; I've been on them, too. Don't tell me how great your sex life is; I can lie, too!*

On the other hand, I've had two hip replacements—three hip *operations*, however, because the first one was to remove a cyst from my hip, replacing it with bone from my pelvis. That was the most torturous pain I ever felt. Never go to a hospital on a holiday, for they are understaffed then, and I was at Columbia Presbyterian for Easter. In those days pain medication was nothing like it is today. It is not an exaggeration to say that, upon waking from the anesthesia, I wanted to die. I had the first hip done in 1984 and the second two years later, which, in comparison, employing the new non-invasive procedure, was a piece of cake; I walked out of the hospital the same day and taught Pilates and yoga less than two weeks later, never feeling any pain! It was because of these hospital experiences that I consider nurses and aides almost more important than the doctors. My grievance is with the quality of aftercare when one is helpless and suffering.

The operations didn't stop our penchant for hiking, an integral part of our lives, and it pleases me to see our children and grandchildren adopting it, too.

Al's soaring career took hold about that time. We built our dream home in fancy Woodcliff Lake, New Jersey, complete with a state-of-the-art media room (one of the first anywhere), a very large above-ground gym in the basement complete with rings to work out on, an art room for me, a pool for the kids, and numerous other rooms, many with fireplaces. The house sat on the crest of a small mountain with a deck that we had built around an immense oak tree. In the winter we had a decent view of New York City. The house featured a bridge to the front door over a lovely pond and water fountain, with lily pads and five *koi* fish our five children had given us as a gift. It was our dream house but, I'm afraid, not the children's. Unlike the Closter house, this one was rather isolated, with few kids around, and those not their types. In fact, Carla resented the high school she had to attend because she thought the kids were either "JAPs or jocks," and she was neither. So she convinced us to take her out of the school, and we enrolled her in a great prep school, the Berkshire School, in Massachusetts.

Another vignette: A couple of years after Carla went there,

SINGING LIGHT

while I was taking a nap one afternoon, I was awakened by a phone call. The woman identified herself with a name that sounded Italian (it ended with an "o"), but I was groggy and didn't quite catch it. She said she wanted to send her daughter to Berkshire, and could I give it a recommendation. I extolled the place. In the course of the conversation, I explained why we'd sent our daughter there. "Carla isn't a JAP or a jock," I said. It wasn't until the second after I hung up that it occurred to me that, even though her last name ended with an "o", the woman's accent and last name was not Italian, but Japanese!

Still, most of those years in Woodcliff Lake hummed with countless pool parties, our huge annual Christmas Eve bashes, and all the holidays, Christian and Jewish included. (But been there done that too many times; I'm relieved I don't have to throw them anymore. When we moved into our Piermont, New York, home after Woodcliff Lake, I converted what would have been the dining room into an extra study. I was done with big dinners. That's what our kids are for now.)

But if things got too ordinarily peaceful, one could always count on remnants of the old Sondra to stir things up. It is my contention that no matter how great one's marriage is, even if you are a *perfect* mate, the one thing you can't be is "different." It's human nature for people to develop a measure of ennui after many years of sameness, even if it's perfection. So periodically I'd try to stoke the fires.

One evening Al and I, coming back from a party in the city, had an enormous argument the subject of which now eludes me. I was so angry that, at the Columbus Circle stoplight, the intersection adjacent to the entrance to Central Park, I threw open the car door and marched straight toward the park. It was midnight. Central Park. Crazy, wild, redheaded woman, alone. Al tore out of the car and tackled me to the ground. Two burly cops appeared, but before they could handcuff Al he did some fast talking with me backing him up, so they let us go, shaking their heads and rolling their eyes, sighing, "Marriage!" Ain't love grand?

Another time, to spice things up, I told Al to meet me after work for a drink at a local hotel in our neighborhood. Inured to my *mishegas*, he agreed. He didn't know that I had decided to punk him by buying a blonde wig, a whole new outfit, and test him by seeing if he would flirt with a strange blonde at the bar. I wish I could describe the look on his face when he *did* give her the once over but, after a beat, realizing *she* was *me*, his double-take was beyond priceless! After chastising him for ogling the blonde, I handed him a key to a room there that I'd previously booked. (!)

He really had the patience of Job with me, though. I suppose one could construe as unreasonable the times I woke him in the middle of the night, once to yell at him to complain of our bed, "You're in my middle!" another in the wee hours of the morning (I must have been dreaming) to demand, "Why are you *ignoring* me!" He awoke and remained awake, wondering what he'd done wrong, while I fell sound asleep again. Another time I was very annoyed about something and told him, "You're so square! Why can't you be like Cary Grant?" As wonderful as Al was again, he was at heart rather conservative and could be a touch square, my fair-haired, sweet, grown-up boy scout. That day I was feeling peevish about who knows what and had a momentary Jones for someone dark and sinister. Al didn't get mad but just ignored my ranting: Who listens to a barking dog? The next day a delivery boy came to our front door with a dozen roses and a card that read *I love you, Cary.* He deserved a medal but earned my undying respect and love.

One night during a romantic dinner celebrating my birthday, I remember telling him some fateful words: how *happy* I was. I would learn to wonder what's up about my birthday and the *H* word, and the superstitious Hungarian in me would live to regret ever saying it, for giving myself a *gri gri* (New Orleans for Jinx). The next day it came.

Renee, Al's sister and only sibling, had lived a charmed life with her husband Norm, a top dog at the National Security Agency, and their three children, Kathy, Cindy, and Jimmy. Norm could never tell us what he did at the office, but we always checked with him first when planning on a trip abroad. (Only once did he warn us off of a planned trip. That was when Qaddafi was in power, up to something no good I guess. At the time we were slated to go to Cannes on one of our biannual business visits. I chickened out, but Al went anyway, and I was miserable the entire time he was gone.)

After breakfast one morning, their daughter, fifteen-year-old Kathy, said goodbye to meet her ride to high school. Renee got a phone call an hour later. Kathy's boyfriend, driving his Volkswagen while smoking pot, had collided with a truck. His car's windshield wiper pierced Kathy's trachea, killing her.

The devastating impact on our family was profound. Renee and I had been very tight. I considered her my dearest friend. Our whole family was extremely distraught. At the funeral home for

Kathy, Renee needed to visit the ladies room, and I accompanied her there. We were in the two stalls side by side when I heard her sigh. There are no words to describe the sound of that sigh.

A few years later she developed breast cancer, which she blamed on the stress of losing Kathy, and eventually died of it.

Dazed with sorrow, we were by coincidence at the same funeral home when Nana, Renee's crazed-with-grief mother, asked me to accompany her to the same ladies room, and we wound up in the same stalls. She too was silent except for uttering the very same sigh.

For a long time after, "a normal life" was what other people had.

THE SECOND THING THAT HAPPENED was Al needing a double bypass. Too sad! Time to change the channel.

We: Part Four

When Al first left movie production to join George Gould in the video business, since they both quite frankly believed in nepotism, hiring many of their friends' relatives (and giving a start to some fairly successful people today), they believed in encouraging their employees to live a healthy life. So they offered membership in a gymnastics class, and, during lunch hour, Al, George, and others went there several times a week. At our home in Woodcliff Lake, we also installed rings in the spacious above-ground basement with wall-to-wall mat covering. Al and George also belonged to an executive medical group that examined them, from head to toe, annually, so we thought we had The Healthy Life covered.

And they were definitely in the fast lane toward success. They were considered pioneers in their field for, among other things, having been first to bring movies into home video and holding the patent on it. (It was the prototype for those big movie dispensers you see outside today's supermarkets.) Videocassettes could also be mailed directly to homes for rent or sale.

Extenuating circumstances—of which I have no recall, because I was not that interested—forced them to sell the patent. Much of what Al did, though interesting to most people, was not that interesting to me, and I now regret not having paid more attention. I wasn't interested in the bones of his business. He'd go to some lengths describing the deals, but my brain discarded the details, and all the people I could have asked who really knew are also gone.

I do recall, however, how intoxicating that period was. I sat in, or was privy to, some exciting deals. For example, we *almost* partnered with Viacom (way before Sumner Redstone came on the scene), and *almost* made a deal that would have put us on the map of history had he not lost a vital bid to Ted Turner's superior library, which then made possible the latter's great fortune, leading to CNN and the rest. I'd hear Al talk about the deals, and my heart would soar or plunge. I was not only oblivious but too sensitive to withstand the tension.

But what was too tense for me was not so for Al. That's the deal with entrepreneurs: He ate Win Some, Lose Some for breakfast. When he came home to tell sizzling tales about his dealings with affluent, high-octane honchos like corporate raiders Mike Milliken, Carl Icahn, or Ron Perelman, I'd be entranced but suffer greatly with nervousness *for* him (though I hid it well) and cheered him on to high heaven.

There was no doubt that he had succeeded in his chosen profession. One evening, a group of our dear friends sat around celebrating Al's achievements, everyone making toasts. When it was Hesh's turn, he lifted his glass of champagne and announced, "I'd

SINGING LIGHT

like to make this toast to Sondra. Not only did she make it possible for Al to be a success, she made it necessary!"

Ouch.

ONE DAY AL CAME HOME WITH A NEW VIDEOCASSETTE to show us. Nina and I sat in our media room (the walls of which I'd covered in carpeting). As Al inserted the cassette into the player, he explained the new concept: watching while listening to music being played. What did we think about it? I said, "It'll never go!" Who would want to distract from the pleasure of music by having to look at stuff at the same time? Of course he didn't listen to me, and, consequently, Teletronics—with studio and technicians—enabled MTV to happen.

Teletronics, and its editors and editing rooms, were hailed in the industry as a template and prototype. Some of their tech stuff was unprecedented, considered the most innovative, and copied worldwide. Specializing in production and post-production, Teletronics was responsible for many shows, including the popular program *This Week in Baseball*, the Roger Kahn video of his *Boys of Summer*, and that exercise one for Debby Reynolds (with whom we became friends for a while), to name a few. Soon, with Sony, they co-founded the first and world's largest duplicating company (Video Corporation of America), which would eventually merge with Technicolor.

The many things *I* did to participate in the company (as substitute personnel manager, receptionist, etc.) included being a gofer, and one of the chores was outrageously Above and Beyond. Marie Schlagel, George and Al's right-hand woman, was in charge of almost everything in the office. She received complaints from the editors that the one thing *not* so wonderful about the editing rooms was a strange odor emanating from the air ducts. Nobody could figure out how to eliminate or correct it. Marie had the idea of introducing vaginal spray into the ducts, and it seemed to work. Whom did she turn to? *Moi.*

I had to go to a drug store and order as many vaginal sprays as I could. I was living at the time in Squaresville— Closter. But good soldier that I was, I trooped right into the local drugstore and cheerfully asked the manager, with whom I had a customer–manager relationship, to order me a large supply of vaginal spray.

He looked at me totally askance. "I'm having a busy week-end," I said.

He looked even more aghast, and although he did order the supply, I never could go into that drugstore again without, as we Markims used to say, less than a modicum of trepidation.

IN 1996 AL WAS INDUCTED INTO THE VIDEO HALL OF FAME. But his big break—when he finally got what he called fuck-you money, came when Ron Perelman bought Teletronics for a handsome sum on the condition that Al, who was its president (George Gould had retired) also run Perelman's various West Coast holdings under the name MacAndrew and Forbes, which included, among many others, Four Star Television. Perelman wanted Al to live in California, but true-blue New Yorker Al refused. It could have been a deal breaker, but Al was a tough poker player, and he prevailed. He agreed he would live bi-coastally (first-class airline tickets and expenses covered). We knew some people who owned a duplex *pied á terre* in Beverly Hills, and we subletted it for one week a month (complete with a Mercedes Benz for me to use) and were set. Several times a year we had to go to either Cannes or some other European venue on business. Tacking on pleasure trips as well, we not only accumulated a gazillion airline miles but got to see the world.

It all sounds lovely, but if I am to adhere to the rules of an honest memoir, it behooves me to include a wart or two.

In the over half a century of Al and my marriage, at least two incidents cut close to the edge, the catalyst usually my old demons. The insecurities deep in me would occasionally rise up, and their fertile soil was, ironically, marriage itself. Al was never boring, but participating in the sameness of marriage, the day-in and day-out of it, buttressed by my incessant need for excitement, fed trouble. The thrill junky I had been as a younger person would occasionally flare in the form of flirting for new conquests. I'd need the rush . . .a hard habit to kick.

Twice this caused a serious dent in our marital bliss. One time it manifested in my obsession over my writing class teacher. Nothing came of that, but enough so that it caused a temporary rupture. Al was perceptive enough to sense my distancing and begged for "transparency." It was short-lived, though, and we got through it.

(I should insert here that Al was not beyond occasionally succumbing to women flirting with him, but as far as I know it didn't amount to anything. But who ever really knows? Great marriages don't necessarily preclude dalliances. We had a *pied á terre* at the Excelsior on Second and Fifty-ninth in Manhattan, and occasionally, if Al had to work very late, he slept there himself. I doubt he was ever unfaithful, since we were united at the hip, but I couldn't swear to it.)

The second time didn't hurt our marriage *per se* but affected my life even worse than if it had. What started as a drunken lark, kidding-around thing erupted into a nightmare. One evening we were with good friends with whom we frequently spent a Saturday night drinking and dining—the former being the operative word. They were seriously serial drinkers, and nobody forced us to keep up (or down) with them. He, a judge, and she, a playwright, were fun people and kind of cute.

One evening, we were zonked out of our heads and started flirting with each other's spouses. Al and she were in one room and the judge and I in the foyer, hugging each other and being silly. I know for certain nothing more would come of it, but the moment he kissed me, the front door opened and in walked our teenage daughter Carla. She looked stricken, immediately turned around, and ran back out, with me too stunned to explain. In the moment it took me to sober up and realize the awful reality of the situation trying to run after her, she was gone.

She eventually came home, and time ameliorated the schism, but it took a long while. I know for a fact we weren't the only happily married couple who fantasized or experimented at the edges, but it was flirting, not fucking. Nothing like that ever happened again, nor did it hurt our solid marriage. But at the time, it hurt our daughter, and that I will always regret.

Another profound moment regarding Carla happened when she was a thirteen-year-old. She came home from a party tipsy.

My perfect, precious child, drunk! Of course, with the role model she had as a mother! I vowed never to touch another drop of alcohol again and didn't for well over a year. It was not as hard as giving up smoking, and I was doing smugly well until a girlfriend convinced me that champagne "wasn't so alcohol-y," and I acquiesced, believing it was a reasonable compromise if I drank only wine and not hard liquor.

I BELIEVE TWO FACTORS CONTRIBUTED to preventing Al from dying of a heart attack at that time.

One was my brother-in-law Bill, who *did* have one, putting enough of a scare into Al to incorporate a brisk pre-work walk into his daily routine. Our house in Woodcliff Lake was surrounded by steep hills.

One morning, as he plodded up one, he had to stop because of a pain in his chest. When it happened again the next day, it was enough to galvanize him to see a cardiologist—leading to open-heart surgery and a double bypass.

For the second factor, I must give kudos to my dear friend Joy, who suggested Al look into a new cardiologist she'd heard of on the West Coast, Dean Ornish. He had developed the radical idea that one could *reverse* heart disease through diet, exercise, and other factors—rather unheard-of at the time, especially within the staid and conservative East Coast medical establishment that typically relied on medicine alone. We went to Berkeley, California, for a week-long seminar with Dr. Ornish that included lectures on yoga, meditation, the adoption of a new diet, and shared support during group therapy sessions, along with some eminent people such as Ben Spock and his wife Mary, with whom we became friends. (It was a hoot learning about the personal and intimate life of the man who'd been my guru when I was a young mother and whose book on childcare had been my sole support in the care of Gary. I'd hardly known anyone in New York except Al, and had virtually no contact with my family in Chicago, with whom I seldom spoke, so his book had become my bible.)

During our session in Oakland, I had the idea of continuing this support regimen by bringing it home and incorporating it into our lives on a regular basis. We acquired a list of people living in our vicinity, hired a facilitator, and we not only found a large, enthusiastic, and faithful group, but those monthly sessions—taking turns at each of our homes—lasted nearly thirty years! Many in our group, including Al and me, credited it for their longevity, and I still maintain that it kept Al alive long past his preordained sell-by date.

Thanks to the Perelman deal, we were able to buy a winter home in La Jolla, California, an oceanfront condo. Falling asleep to the sound of waves, reveling in the extraordinary beauty of the area and the superb weather, made for a fabulous addition to our joy. We also bought a small boat Al named the *Sonjili* (Sonjlloveyou), which had been a lifelong dream for me. I felt very fortunate.

Eventually Al retired, but it was premature. He was only in his late sixties and still felt vital, albeit middle-aged. Knowing how retirement would be anathema to him, for he wasn't a golfer, fisherman, or tennis player, I felt it prudent to head off any predictable *agita* by suggesting he get involved in something, and that something turned out to be local politics, which sustained him for a short time. I can't remember in what capacity he involved himself because it wasn't too interesting to me, but it couldn't have been very noteworthy. He soon segued into pursuing, and managing to pass, the New York Arbitrage Association requirements, and enjoyed becoming an *arbitrageur* for a spell. After that, at my prodding, he became the president of our community's home association, which he ran expertly and, with his math brain, saved some homeowners a great deal of money by successfully suing the county. (Al could have been a superb lawyer, and in fact Ron Perelman's personal lawyer once asked Al to look over his own renewal contract before he signed it.)

The other thing Al did around then was create a program, with the New York State office of AARP, that he called Second-Half Strategies. Produced at MNN in New York, it was devoted to the second half of life, a series of half-hour shows relating to the interests of seniors. I too volunteered my services producing shows and interviewing on camera a great many interesting celebrities as well as non-celebrities. (A few notables: Steve Allen, Pete Seeger, Bud Greenspan, Ed Koch, and Celeste Holm.) The show ran for a number of years under Al's guidance and, as of this writing, is still producing. In fact, if you're curious to see us, look up *Sex and the Senior* on YouTube. One of the producers was looking for a viable couple for her show. Among other things, it was revealed that, in comparison to the waning effects of aging, there were a few times when our lovemaking was six times a day. *When we were younger*, I hasten to add! In those days, like other young people in love, we couldn't get enough of each other. Night, day—

the word "naps" had a different meaning in our family. Ask our kids. "God Love him," as Nana might say! And I did and I did and I did.

In the meantime, as I've mentioned, I started teaching Pilates and yoga for a small group of women in our neighborhood. I was motivated to do so because I couldn't find the type of classes locally that I'd enjoyed in La Jolla, so, having taken notes from the La Jolla classes, I hung out my shingle as it were in Piermont (initially, at no charge until I got it down). Eventually, I got licensed.

At my prodding, Al formed a group of men who met once a month at a local restaurant to discuss a topic anyone chose. They called themselves "The Romeos"—Retired Older Men Eating Out. We'd heard about another group who had done that too, and putting this one together was very gratifying for Al.

For a long time, Al and I did this little tango, combining our charities with a lively social life, which sustained us quite nicely. Emblematic of my maturation and ability to settle down, I went from blazing red hair to old-lady blonde. No longer edgy and quick-tempered, I finally felt comfortable enough in my own skin to eschew my need to prove something. With the old Peggy Lee demon disappearing, I found myself seeing value in things other than the shallow ones that had once pleased me. I clearly remember how I used to scoff at people happy with simply having dinner at a restaurant. My old instincts had been to get done with dinner and go somewhere—a disco, party, or bar, and have *fun!* I became one of those square people who truly relished a good meal, especially with good friends, who could actually love hiking in the woods or visiting loved ones or seeing a movie while holding hands.

It might offer some hope to my progeny if they ever worry about getting older that, in my case anyway, life has grown more content as I've aged. It grew, after thirty, exponentially with each decade. Though one could never describe me as docile and free of emotional scars, Al's consistent love overcame most of the demons of my childhood. That must have taken herculean patience and speaks to his ability, self-confidence, and the unshakeable knowledge that he was truly loveable—compliments of his upbringing. The dynamics of Al's placid and uncomplicated persona playing against my quixotic, skittish one didn't prevent us from finding our rhythm and a lifestyle intrinsic to our temperaments, one that made room for the yin–yang of us, and lasted over five decades. Can I get an amen?

We were aware of Al's predisposition to cardiovascular disease because his symptoms were becoming more apparent despite diligently adhering to his Ornish diet. No matter what, his seventyish-year-old body kept producing plaque. He had to have an operation on his eye once, so clogged up were its tiny arteries. Many of our peers, including Herbie and Hesh, had died, and others were nearly there. We counted ourselves extremely fortunate having lived as long as we had and so well. We felt he had cheated death by adhering strongly to the Ornish regimen, and that our time on earth together, relatively healthy in our sixties and seventies, was a bonus. So we walked the walk, which, given my propensity for living in that Egyptian River Denial, was easy for me.

I prided myself on being ultra-realistic and discussed our what-ifs. We agreed that, whichever of us went first, we would hope the other, if they chose and were able to, could find another mate. We cheerfully scouted funeral homes so we could save our children the hassle. (I wrote an article called "Shopping to Die For," describing various establishments that we checked out. It was published in the *Bergen Record*, a highly reputable newspaper, and one may find it online if one's so inclined.)

Seven years older than me, Al was by then in his eighties. I noticed changes in his memory. An extremely articulate man with a masterful command of language, he started prefacing sentences with "uh." Words were, it became apparent, no longer easily at his disposal. My radar alerted, I felt maybe it was time for him to quit being the president of the homeowner's association. Time to stop striving and *efforting* so much. I also began worrying about his driving, though I ascribed some of his imperfections to the usual ravages of old age. (I realize now I was in denial.) I started driving more.

The dawning realization that Al was changing seeped into my brain like ice on teeth. The disintegration was gradual enough to feed into my denial, but it eventually became clear that life, as we knew it, would soon be no more. His cognition was like a leaking boat, slowly decomposing into oblivion. It was helpful to us both for him to attend a senior center, one especially good for people in Al's condition. I had to leave written messages for him, reminding him to do brush his teeth, shower, that the center's bus would be picking him up that day, and that the clothes he needed to dress in were on the chair. When he couldn't handle those chores, I had to increase my aid. However, he still had cognitive reason at that time.

One year was particularly torturous for me. While he was in this state, Gary suffered what is called mid-life crisis, and the Mother Bear in me kicked in as much as the Wife Bear. Leaving Al for a few days was difficult, but I did it, going back and forth to where Gary lived to try to help. Even Danny flew out to California to assist. Eventually Gary recovered completely, but during that time I thought of myself as a sad sandwich.

Not much afterwards, I was diagnosed with grade one ductal carcinoma. I had a lumpectomy, and Gary rallied to step up to the plate for me, accompanying me and seeing me through the operation. It turned out to be minor, thankfully. You can't even see a scar. I never did radiation or chemo or anything, just had frequent mammograms. Happily I've been discharged to once-a-year mammos.

THEN CAME MAY 16, 2011, MY BIRTHDAY. *What is it about my birthday?*

The day before, we had done something unprecedented. Even though we had both been actors, we had never performed together, except at UCSD School of Continuing Education drama class in La Jolla a few years earlier, where, unashamedly, we enjoyed being a big deal because everyone made a huge fuss over us: "The Markims, professional actors from New York!" I cajoled Al into doing something in New York for friends and family. (It turned out, ironically, to be *Love Letters*.) We must have made a good impression here also, since we got a standing ovation, but, uncharacteristically, he had messed up a few lines, for which I had to cover him with nobody but me knowing. Clearly, he wasn't at his best.

The next day, May 16, at cocktail hour, we were sitting in our living room enjoying a glass of wine, just chilling, as was our custom. We would call it *oeinasana* (*asana* is a Sanscrit word for a "pose," and we added the *oein*, the Greek word for "wine".) Feeling content and mellow, we began talking about plans to celebrate my birthday.

Suddenly, out of nowhere, his words became gibberish like a drunk's, and his eyes went dead. How I guessed that he might be having a stroke, I don't know. Stunned and paralyzed at first, I somehow knew he had to get to a hospital, and my automatic pilot kicked me swiftly into action.

The rest was three years of hell.

ONE HEARS ABOUT THESE THINGS—tragedy striking—and perhaps one thinks one can mentally prepare for all contingencies. It's not true. People praise me, asking how I could have kept him at home and done all the care-taking I did for all those years. The simple answer is you don't know how strong you can be until you have to be. I read something once by a guy named Josh Shipp:

> *You either get better or you get bitter. It's that simple. You either take what's been dealt to you and allow it to make you a better person or you allow it to tear you down. The choice does not belong to fate. It belongs to you.*

In-your-face reality.

Me: Part One

> "It takes courage to grow up
> and become who you really are."
> —e.e. cummings

IN REVIEWING WHAT I'VE WRITTEN thus far, an ungenerous reader might construe much of it as regurgitated negativity, as though writing could expiate, exorcise, or cauterize those agonizing times in a confessional memoir. When I told some friends I wanted to write and bare all, one of them asked, "You're going to air your dirty laundry in public? Maybe because I'm Irish," she added, "but I could never do that! Why do you want to, Sondra?"

Good question. Why be subjected to judgment and criticism? When I awoke the next morning, before I even opened my eyes, the answer was clear. To her "Why do that, Sondra?" I thought, *Why not? All of my history has made me who I am today, and I'm a good person.* Perhaps I can convey the lessons I've learned while giving my life meaning. Obviously I'm not happy about, but also not embarrassed by, my life's afflictions. They cannot be erased but, within the chaos of whatever pain and rage I endured, growth, authenticity, and joy have followed, so I offer myself as proof they can.

And yes, of course the ameliorating process toward healing is in play as well.

I admit it's easier to describe people and events with a broad brush. And perhaps I'm unconsciously skewing my history through my own biased perceptions. (It saves time and effort to condense.) But in the spirit of full transparency, I admit people are not one-dimensional heroes or villains. Although my parents imposed a toll of emotional tyranny on me, my mother was not all Cruella. Even my stepfather had his moments—such as the time or two he interceded on my behalf when Mother was beating me. And though the incestuous moves on me were horrendous, they were never got past touching and were only very occasional. And hell, he never hurt me *physically*. I lacked luxuries, but I always had a roof over my head and food on the table. I didn't have cashmere sweaters, but I did have woolen ones. And I'm grateful to my parents for two things: good genes, and the ricocheting motivation to develop empathy and be better than them.

And Jack Shelton was, at least, my college education and fabulously adventurous. (One event sticks out in my mind. Before we married that May, he wanted a couple of days after Christmas to show me New York, especially on New Year's Eve. Our plan was to hear Midnight Mass at St. Pat's and join the hullabaloo in Times Square. We set off from Chicago in the little MG and began the long slog. Halfway into Indiana, snow started coming down relentlessly, and the windshield wipers stopping working altogether. Jack had to roll down the window, stick his head out every few minutes, and try to drive that way, periodically stopping to wipe at his face and eyes. It became impossible to go any further, but we were in the middle of nowhere—not a town in sight, just a few farmhouses. "Pick a house," he said. I chose the one with the nicest Christmas tree. We parked, knocked on their door, and explained our plight. They generously invited us to stay the night. It was a lovely evening. God takes care of drunks, fools, and the young! I doubt one could do that today.)

ALL FIVE OF MY PARENTS HAVE DIED, as has my sister Eileen. My mother lived to be ninety-four (and died of natural causes), Art died in his eighties (from colon cancer), and Jack Robinson in his seventies (I'm taking poetic license and saying the cause was sheer evil). Eileen, an incessant smoker, died in her early seventies of emphysema. The only funerals that truly pained me were Eileen's, Renee's, and Kathy's. As for my parents, there was the stinging reality that I no longer had a buffer. I'm reminded of the wonderful Gerald Manley Hopkins poem:

> *Márgarét, áre you gríeving*
> *Over Goldengrove unleaving?*
> *Leáves like the things of man, you*
> *With your fresh thoughts care for, can you?*
> *Ah! ás the heart grows older*
> *It will come to such sights colder*
> *By and by, nor spare a sigh*
> *Though worlds of wanwood leafmeal lie;*
> *And yet you will weep and know why.*

> *Now no matter, child, the name:*
> *Sórrow's springs áre the same.*
> *Nor mouth had, no nor mind, expressed*
> *What heart heard of, ghost guessed:*
> *It ís the blight man was born for,*
> *It is Margaret you mourn for.*

It took me some time to understand that. What I've come to comprehend is that, when we mourn at funerals, we cry, not only for the dearly departed, but for ourselves.

At my mother's funeral the word "next" resounded implicitly, yet I felt no great sadness. But if ever it was myself I mourned for, it was at my husband's.

> *Once you become real you can't become unreal*
> *Again. It lasts for always. . .and you cannot be*
> *Ugly, except to people who don't understand.*
> —The Velveteen Rabbit

As I've mentioned, aside from yoga, which I've taught for twenty years, I ran a memoir class. Initially, I had no intention of writing my own but something caught fire, became a catalyst, and words happened. When I sat down to write seriously, I was surprised how easily self-absorption unlocked recall. The process of writing itself grew to become my *ikigai*, a Japanese word meaning "purpose or reason for being," so my life spilled into words with a sort of vengeance. Perhaps it's preparation to vent the following.

I thought the traumas heretofore chronicled were unbearable.

They pale beside losing Al. So now the blackest period of all.

Having had enough "warning" time, I may have thought I had a few years to gird myself for his impending death, but I didn't take into account the full extent of the effect or emotional cost of his insidious *decline* that left me emptied out, with a feeling like being irrevocably halved.

That brilliant man, who once had had occasion to say, "Ontogeny recapitulates phylogeny," could not come up with the word for "shoe." I had once watched as he commandeered an auditorium full of Wall Street powerhouse makers and breakers, analysts and investors, dazzling them with his profound knowledge, compelling charisma, and sense of humor. From the moment he took the stage, you knew he was the real deal, and he had you at "Good afternoon."

But from May 16, 2011, until his death on November 24, 2015, our life as I knew it vanished.

I am aware of the futility of attempting to extinguish the need for *Life As It Was*—but I'm still working hard to weave the prosthesis for a new one.

That requires fully accepting and thereby processing all that happened. I could describe the day-by-day diminishment his vascular dementia exacted, but, frankly, I'm loath to put myself through that again. It's still too raw—as of this writing, not quite two years later.

To give you an idea, a day comes to mind when I was grappling with the local tax office in my county, which had penalized me several hundred dollars for being a few days late paying our bill. Pleas fell on deaf ears. I begged, Please, I had never paid our bills before, my husband was incapacitated, we had never been late in over twenty years, and so on, to no avail. I kept persisting until they finally agreed the man in charge would consider and get back to me that day. Hours went by. I was sorting out the countless pills Al needed into the weekly pill dispenser when the doorbell rang.

It was the mailman, with a package of the various creams, toilet wipes, diapers, and protective bed mats from Drugstore.com. Oh, and my mail—including another bill claiming a penalty charge for tardiness.

I see me now, holding the new bill in my hand, when at that moment Al indicates he needs bathroom call. Whenever he does that, I go into warp speed to unbuckle, unbutton, dismantle, and push him faster to the toilet STAT. I barely make it, but with letter still in hand, I set him down. It's a false alarm. Par for the course.

I no sooner get him settled to "give it time" when the phone rings. It's the tax people, and as I say hello, Al makes urgent noises, calling me. Still talking, I rush back to find him half standing and grunting. I try to resettle him and, sparing details, I'll just say that, with the new bill and phone still in my hand, and as I deal with their rejection of my plea, the other hand gets caught under Al just as his fickle bowels decide to work. Caught red-handed!

It was a moment of instant challenge to what I was made of. A call to arms of sorts—(the fastidious, picky me—I won't even drink from anyone's glass; changing my children's or grandchildren's diapers required a mask)—or *Mench*-it-up time!

I like to think the latter. I know I dug deep in my heart for all the love and tenderness I felt for that good, beautiful soul, but it was a bitch of a day that left me a wreck. And that was only one of them.

Interspersed with the challenges were countless falls, constant wanderings. One day in particular, he got lost at a mall. It was during the early phase of his dementia, and I didn't yet realize the extent of his failing. The details aren't important except to say that our grandson Josh and I scoured the mall (the second largest in the country) for three hours until the police found him.

People ask what happened to him. What happened was largely genetic. He had a propensity for cardio-vascular problems, and he was in his eighties. His slide downhill started in the hospital he'd gone to for a minor ailment, where he contracted a nightmare infection called C-Dif. It's like a MIRSA. In my opinion, anytime elderly people (who almost by definition often have compromised immune systems) enter a hospital, they come out on the wrong end of healthy. We've all read about those with Alzheimer's. Their condition appears similar, but in Al's case, the vascular dementia was less debilitating, in that he was never hostile or lashed out. His body was ruined, but his soul was intact. Frustrated and exasperated that he couldn't express what he was feeling, yes—but the biggest debit was his being so terribly lost. He didn't know where, what, who, why. He still loved singing patriotic songs and smiled a lot. He pretty much recognized his family until the end, and he always knew me, never stopped telling me in his slurred babble-language that he loved me, but from that day in May when his luck gave out, my husband was no more.

As I've said, I was his caregiver, doing everything a caregiver does: feeding, cleaning, including the onerous toilet activities—diapering, shaving, driving to doctors, more doctors, and more doctors, endlessly and assiduously sorting out and giving him his countless pills, walking him, first with a cane, then his walker, and then in his wheelchair. Also massaging, soothing (screaming), hugging, kissing, and singing to him. He wouldn't let me leave him for respite. He wouldn't go to sleep unless I tucked him in and sang and played his favorite Yo-Yo Ma. And, again, I also had to assume all his duties—the bookkeeping, bills, running the household. I had never done any of that before, because he had kept me in a bubble (or pumpkin shell): He liked being a leader, and I enjoyed not having to deal with anything, to the extent that he drove everywhere, paid for everything, and made almost every decision. I never even brought a purse with me when we went out.

Another cold glass of reality thrown in my face occurred in La Jolla. I was trying to handle our finances when we weren't otherwise immersed in the pleasures of the place. Sitting on the beach, I got a call on my cell from our Fidelity man. "Mrs. Markim, you are eating into your margin." I was doing *what* to my *what*? That happened twice, and each time they forgave my blunder by forgiving the penalty. The third time they suggested I get a money manager. I hate to think how much money I wasted on various penalties.

But fear, anger, desperation, frustration, and helplessness were nothing compared to dealing with the fraud sitting in the wheelchair with Al's skin and smell, who spoke in Al's voice, wearing his face and lips that I had once drawn sustenance from. This imposter elicited nothing but pity and annoyance, combined with guilt and despair. It got so bad one particularly egregious time that I was driven to the point of seriously contemplating suicide, and even getting us into the car to careen into a wall or river. I actually started to do it but chickened out at the last minute. That was my life then.

He liked me to massage his back. Once, after his morning wash and before putting on his pajamas, I took some soothing ointment and began rubbing it all over, from his shoulders to the edge of his Pampers. His sighs spurred me past the moles and protruding bones—this back, once so broad and strong and sometimes, when the intensity carried me away, scratched by passion, this very back, the one I first held while dancing on the River Queen a gazillion years before.

There was no assuaging the ambiguous loss of my brilliant partner and lover. I felt rudderless. But I tried to reboot my emotions, lecture myself: *Hey, I scored the best years of my life for over fifty-five years with this man. We kept the music playing! How many people can say that? And who am I to think it would go on forever? Am I so entitled to being impervious to misfortune?* I'm reminded of the crude old joke about hillbillies isolated from females when, one day, the adolescent brother tells his older ones he's feeling horny and what should he do. They take him to a barrel with a hole in it and tell him to insert his thang into the hole. He loves it. It's great. He repeats this daily until one day he's told, "Not today. It's your turn in the barrel."

I USED TO JOKE TO PEOPLE that our grandparents had no time to be neurotic. Without, for example, washing machines, they were so busy making a living and a home that they didn't have time for such luxuries. When I look back on that dismal time with caring for Al, I realize that I too, had no time to be anything but caring. It was more than a full-time job. Without even taking the complex logistics of caretaking into account, each moment seemed to demand my attention. A small example: There were times when Al would slip off his wheelchair, and I couldn't prevent him from falling to the floor or lift him off it by myself. I had to call in the marines, more specifically the police or, as once happened in La Jolla, when I couldn't get him out of the bathtub, firemen. And there are thirty steps from my bedroom to where he was in the finished basement that I climbed at least eight times a day! These demands so filled my mind that I think a bit of me grew emotionally. Childish Sondra was, gradually, growing up. I was filled with a sense of caring and determined to make the rest of his life the best it could be. I had to authentically assess what was important to me. Could I continue living this interrupted, difficult life? Changing his diapers? Sacrificing? I'd been advised, even by his own doctor, to put him in a home that cared for people in his position. But I couldn't. I had to keep him with me.

I finally consulted a therapist who, against my deep resistance, convinced me to get on Lexapro; it at least helped me sleep. My children convinced me to get help, so I hired a full-time live-in caretaker, and we rearranged the lower level and bathroom there. Because Al was a veteran, we received help in the form of part-time aides and supplies, even a moveable chair to transport Al from the lower floor to the living area. Later, we got hospice as well, truly a lifesaver. He had weekly visits from a massage therapist, a young woman brought her guitar and would play while I sang, and a kind elderly volunteer came to read from whatever book she happened to be reading. She was company even if he didn't comprehend the words. Even with all of that, Al was not content letting me out of his sight. I managed in those years to take two short trips away—one to my favorite place in Utah, a hiking spa, with Nina (whom I've always considered my gift), bonding us even closer. The other was a week-end joining Carla on a business trip to New Orleans, where I could slay ghosts and play host showing her "my city," a big-time treat for me. I would advise anybody in such a leaking boat as I was in, to get away, even if it's for an overnight.

Al's was not the type of dementia, as I have said, in which he was either angry, mean, or totally out of it, though he went through each of those phases momentarily. Sometimes he would balk at going somewhere, like, for example, the senior center. (I lured him there by volunteering to teach chair yoga to the group, which made him happy.) One time in particular we had to go to somewhere important—maybe a family reunion—I'd been planning on for a long time. It was one of those moments where he was being ornery. "No, I don't want to go! I'm sick! I'm not well!" he informed me.

I pleaded with him, trying my usual cajoling tricks, to no avail. Finally I told him, "Listen, Al, you are going to get up, get dressed, and we are going! You can die tomorrow, but we are going today!" And indeed he had a good time, smiling and laughing (albeit in tongues) to everyone!

As the joke goes, I felt as if the light at the end of the tunnel was another train. There were weeks when he had to be in a nursing home (the result of another hospital visit I'd been forced to allow, since he was bleeding externally, setting him back worse than before). After that, I was even more determined to keep him home with me until the end, and no more hospitals no matter what!

ON TOP OF ALL THIS, IT BECAME NECESSARY to sell our dream place in La Jolla because he couldn't travel anymore, and somehow I managed to do it.

I'd walk him around our neighborhood daily, and I found there were some people who leered at him, some curious to see what had happened to the great ship that had gone down, and some quite kind and sweet to him. I'd push his wheelchair around our house to the pier where, we had bought a bench. It's inscribed with our names and reads Paradise Found. (Our community is called Paradise.) He liked sitting there quietly with me, holding hands. During Hurricane Sandy, of the more than dozen benches embedded in cement along the pier, all but two were blown into the river. Ours remained, and you can be sure we spun a metaphor out of that!

One afternoon, holding hands while watching television cartoons (Daniel, our caregiver was also in the room, busy on his iPhone), out of the blue Al looked up at me expectantly, sporting a big grin. At that stage he spoke in a sort of foreign language, some of which I could decipher, so I had paid no attention to him babbling at the TV. Consequently, I was totally taken aback when, this time, he looked at me as though the lights were back on and, clear as day, said, "Son-ra, wanna fuck?" I couldn't believe my ears and glanced incredulously at Daniel. Daniel is a dark-skinned

African American, but I do believe he was turning red laughing as he nodded. Never one to turn down an offer like that, I stood up from my chair and sat on his lap saying, "Sure! Come on!" At that point, whatever lucid light had been in his eyes went out, and he returned to staring at the TV, surprised I was on his lap. I should add here that it was uncharacteristic language for Al—he was never so crude—but then the whole situation was unreal.

It soon became necessary to call in hospice for assistance, because he was rapidly losing altitude. They supervised his treatment more and more as he grew weaker and lesser. My ambivalence was almost absurd: I yearned for the agony to be over but dreaded it even more.

In June, Gary and his pretty fiancée Nancy, both of whom lived in California, very considerately made plans to be married near us so that Al could attend. They arranged the head table at the reception to include them, the bride and groom, and us, along with Daniel. It was a heavenly day for me, one exceedingly needed. There were moments during the ceremony when Al made inappropriate babbling sounds, and some of us grew uncomfortable, but if the bride and groom felt it paramount for Dad to be there and were cool with it, I was, too. Sitting at the head table, Daniel placed the bib on Al and fed him. He also tried to control Al's occasional weird exclamations. At first I was rather self-conscious about how that appeared and sounded, but I tried focusing on the happy occasion, and, reinforced with a couple of glasses of sauvignon blanc, got through it happily.

The next day our clan came to our place for lunch. I learned that one of our children had been extremely embarrassed about

"Dad being exposed the way he had," thinking, If Dad had been in his right mind, he would have felt it undignified and preferred staying home. Yeah! I got that! I also got that I needed a powwow with the kids. Having had plenty of time to reflect on the embarrassing aspects of dementia, I'd truly come to believe there was nothing to be ashamed of. It could happen to anyone—to you, to me—and does, in fact, more than sixty percent of the time, to the elderly. People would have to understand that it was more important for Gary to have his father present and, intuitively, I am convinced that, somewhere deep down, Al enjoyed participating too. I believe they came to agree.

If other people didn't like it, ask me if I care.

SINGING LIGHT

Me: Part Two

I T'S OUT OF SEQUENCE, but about two and a half years earlier we had celebrated our fiftieth wedding anniversary. Al was barely Al then, but at least could still register and communicate enough, though stiltedly and poorly. I knew down deep he was still the old ham he'd always been, and I felt confident he would enjoy, and be up to the task of putting on, a little entertainment for the big party we were planning. I composed a parody of the song, "You'll Never Know" (...just how much I love you, inserting funny tidbits). We rehearsed his part repeatedly. Singing together had always been an integral part of our lives and brought much joy to Al, who, throughout our marriage, constantly begged me to sing to him. It was never a task since I loved to accommodate him and it flattered me that he thought I was Sarah Vaughan incarnate! At our celebration, there was an abundance of friends and family.

It gives me comfort knowing we made it to fifty, still in love. Three years later, the last vestiges of his cognizance, like a setting sun, began to morph into a forever night.

As I've said, I have never been easily given to crying. But if I were so inclined, I'd especially try to refrain from doing so in front of a child or, as in this case, my new child, Al. Only once did I let down in front of him. It's also worth noting, if only to illustrate the soul that still resided in him no matter the ravages of the disease.

That afternoon, sitting with him as I frequently did, it happened that I felt the full brunt of our plight as never before, and it overwhelmed me. I fell onto his lap, sobbing, fully aware that I might as well have been crying on a statue. And he did blithely continue watching television, oblivious. Eventually, I pulled myself together and went on with my day.

Many hours later, feeling somewhat composed, I went back down to him and, though I knew he'd have no idea what I was talking about, told him I was feeling better. Once again he surprised me by looking at me, connecting with *real* eyes, and patted my head. Then, smiling lovingly, he said one clear word: "Good." So it *had* registered. He *had* cared, just couldn't express it at the time. He was always in there somewhere, I believe, even to the end.

Long ago, when we didn't truly *believe* we'd die, we had decided that if, heaven forbid, we *did* die, we'd be cremated, and that, when the first of us died, the ashes would be saved to eventually be mixed with the ashes of the other. We'd ask that part of our combined remains be strewn in our beloved hiking place, Torrey Pines in California, near La Jolla, and the rest in the Hudson River near our Piermont, New York, bench. Or whatever the children decided—it didn't matter because, as I told Al, our souls would meet and be together forever. I hesitate to admit this, knowing how nutty it sounds, but I confess to a childlike consoling fantasy that clings to a hope we have souls and can be together eternally. Al, an atheist, kindly indulged me. I think of myself as agnostic because I do pray before I go to sleep at night and enjoy clinging to the thought that, when we die, *maybe* we'll exist in our souls, and that I can also be an angel to my children and grandchildren. This view of the Hereafter, admittedly, is striped with the narrative of my old fairytale sensibility, which perhaps has never quite left me. Yet if I'm honest and think about it, for an agnostic I sure have no problem trying to summon whoever it is when circumstances require, such as "Oh, please God, let her get home safely," or "Please God, let the diagnosis be negative!" It certainly comforts me knowing my remains will be with his forever.

Another departure from the mature and realistic person I've grown to become is my sobriquet, "Gypsy"—"Hungarian gypsy," to be exact. That started when I was a little girl. We had a dog, Toasty, who got killed by a car. The night before, I'd had had a dream he was dead and told my family of it that day. That was the day *before* he got killed. So they joked that I was a gypsy. When I was a little older, I dreamed that my grandmother had died, and the next day she did. My grandmother *was* elderly (at least seventy-four) and in failing health. But still. . . .

Excavating another anecdote: One weekend Al and I packed up the family and went to visit friends in Westhampton. The next day I told everyone about a dream I'd had that our apartment had been robbed. When we got home, we found my few good pieces of jewelry gone and all of Al's clothes, leaving him with the sole suit he still had at the cleaners. And a few years later, I dreamed one night that John Wayne had died. He did, but it took two years! (That was when I began to question my gypsy intuition.)

But I do believe some people have a keener ESP ability than others, substantiated many times by me and others, my friend Sarah and Danny, in particular. I mention all this because, though it was a given that Al's days were numbered, no one could predict precisely when—it could have been days, weeks, hours.

Yet on the night that he died, I had unprecedentedly intuited it that day, to the extent that I actually crawled up onto his small hospital bed with him, not a thing I usually did. Though an avowed atheist, Al had never renounced his sense of Judaism and lately had been muttering things about God. They say there are no atheists in foxholes, yet years ago, right before Al's double bypass heart operation, when one would have expected him to at least hedge his bet with a *teeny* prayer, he never uttered a word. So I was surprised when now he started making sounds like "God" and talking about his father taking him to *shul* (synagogue) as a boy. Somewhere deep in him, did he sense his impending end, finally in the foxhole?

I cradled him in one arm, my other hand stroking his forehead, and sang the Jewish prayer "*Shma Yisrael*," seeing how it comforted him. Of course I reiterated what I'd said numerous times a day, that I loved, loved, loved him. But this time, I added my thanks for being the best husband a woman could have, for being the better part of me, and by reminding him we'd be together always, silently praying my words would get through to him.

In retrospect, I'm grateful I did. Perhaps it was my closure.

The drama mama in me would like to tell you that, at that point, he smiled, we kissed, the music swelled to a crescendo, and he died in my arms. It didn't happen that way. It would happen unceremoniously later that night, or rather, around four in the morning, while I was sleeping in my bed, not near him, but with the baby monitor near my head.

We used to muse about which date would be our last. November 24, 2015, turned out to be his—and also the day I think of as my amputation.

I take comfort knowing that the aide who cared for him the last couple of months—even better than Daniel had—slept in a bed right next to him. A very light sleeper, she said she knew it was his time by the sounds he made, and she administered his last morphine dose.

She was thoughtful enough not to awaken me until she first cleaned him, combed his hair, and closed his eyes. I recall having heard the sound of splashing water on the monitor in my sleep, but I assumed it was his usual ablutions, so I went back to sleep until she knocked on my bedroom door and I became no longer a person who couldn't cry, leaving behind the person I knew as me.

I'M NOT SURE IF IT WAS when I was ten years old that my playmate Barbara Kranz's mother died, and I saw her dead body in a casket. But it terrorized me and left me numb with a fear of dead bodies. I have never been able to touch one. I wouldn't even look at my mother's when my sisters were attending her at the funeral home and asked me to come say good-bye, nor did I go into the room. I wasn't sure how I'd react to Al's, but when I went down and saw him, without thinking, I ran and collapsed on his hardened body, stroking and kissing his cold face, the sound of aloneness deafening my sobs.

This is a poem I wrote when I was a teenager:

The joke of all this is that we die. We really die.
Is it perhaps a sleep that is forever
But someday we shall never
And you laugh or pass it by, the someday, and don't think of it.
Still someday the someday will really come.
All our lives we worry, try, work become, only to die?
But aren't you jealous, angry too?
The stupid questions will still go on
Like are you Catholic or Jew, and the lipsticks too,
like "Which becomes you?"
And revelations will go on like one and one are two
Yet someday we shall cease to be there, never be there
To see or hear the latest news or gossip
or have a light or heavy heart or pocket
Because our heart will be apart with decay
and whatever happens to the heart and
the rest when pffft, someday comes for real and that's it.

And that was it.

Me: Part Three

THERE ARE TWO TIMES A PERSON DIES: when he does, and when the last person who remembers him does. Two years before Al died, we had been "walking" in our favorite park, near our home in Piermont, at a time when he was still reasonably coherent and could get a thought across. He started mumbling something about not being afraid to die. Our family always recorded everything, starting with old-fashioned movie cameras. We have numerous videos of us taking videos of us as we are taking videos! We have pictures galore of every event and now iPhone videos and FB pictures of each detail of each event! (I even took a picture of Al dead to send to my children so they could "be there," to process and accept the reality and finality—and perhaps because I needed the comfort of their witness.)

Anyway, in the park that afternoon when Al said he wasn't afraid to die, it occurred to me to capture his thoughts, so I whipped out my iPhone and asked him to expound upon the subject. His obvious deterioration notwithstanding, he accommodated me beautifully: He'd lived a good long life, better than he'd hoped...and it was time. I later asked his dearest friend, Manning Ruben—only a year younger than Al but still alive and with all his marbles—for help. They'd known each other from the beginning, maintaining their friendship throughout teenage-hood, wives, schools, starting at U of Penn in 1944, then to VMI and NC State, and through basic training in 1945, sharing experiences in Germany, and keeping it going as long as they could. At Gary's wedding, all of us making speeches to the newlyweds, Manning stood up too and—-in front of Al wearing his bib, withered in his wheelchair, and totally out of it—-made a brilliant speech about the younger, vibrant Al, reminding all of us of the man he had been. I'll love Manning always for that.

So now I'd lean on his tech ability and ask him to burn a DVD of the video for me. And he did, splendidly, even adding music and a perfect visual before and after.

Keep your fingers on that place while I put on my big-girl panties for the funeral.

It was to be held at a charming little church in our town, a Norman Rockwell postcard if ever there was one. We're Jewish; I get that. But (a) there were no temples nearby, (b) we didn't belong to one anyway, and (c) funeral homes were onerous to me and smelled bad.

The reason Al adopted that church after he lost cognizance is not fully clear to me. It's true that our hiking trails surrounded it, and we had once attended a non-denominational sing-along there. It was a quote religious place unquote. If you want to know more, that's all I've got.

But during his last year of life, every time I drove by it he'd throw kisses, saying, "That's my church!" (and get his fingermarks all over the car's glass window, which I've yet to wipe off).

On a whim one day a couple of years before Al died, I had called the pastor there and asked if he would consider having our service; without a pause, he had agreed, so when Al did die, I called again, and we arranged to meet. Accompanied by three of our children, I encountered a handsome young man with a ponytail who turned out to be the pastor (also a musician), and he couldn't have been more accommodating.

The day of the funeral he had, unsolicited, removed all obvious Christian references, and he opened the service with these words: "Why a church?" He offered to some of our surprised guests the reasons I've just given. Then, without prompting, he began singing, in Hebrew, the Jewish prayer for the dead ("*Y'isgadal. . .*") with three of Al's male friends joining in on the finish. I had hired a piano player to play all our favorite songs, it was a full house, including some old employees of Teletronics who had traveled a long way and expounded upon Al being "one of the finest gentlemen," "the best boss," and so on. I trust it all went well; I only recall feeling untethered, truncated, afloat in a fog throughout the service. The thought running through my head was whether I'd ever outrun my grief.

It won't come as a surprise when I say I love to write and pride myself in the capacity to come up with a decent speech if necessary. But atypically of me then, I hadn't prepared a word until the morning of the funeral, and then I only jotted down a few words.

Though I can't remember them, I do recall the words borrowed from my yoga *Contemplations* folder:

> *This is my wish for you. Comfort on difficult days,*
> *Smiles when sadness intrudes,*
> *Love to complete your life.*
> *For in the end what matters most is:*
> *How well did you love*
> *How well did you live   How well did you learn to let go?*

And another, unprecedented, first: There was no video. So I can't add the rest of what I said as I stood on the dais next to Al's urn, which was surrounded by the largest flower arrangement I'd ever seen, compliments of his favorite cousin, Eliott Stahler. Behind it was the American flag folded into its triangle, compliments of the United States Army. But I needn't have worried about what to say, because our five children and a few grandchildren were exquisite in giving their eulogies. One moment stays with me: Ryan spoke my very thoughts when he said, "Papa's not really gone, because he's looking out here at the faces of his family," he said, who are "bits and pieces of him still," and Julie's eulogy brought tears. My grandchildren were *menschen*. In many cases it took extraordinary effort, but come they did! They showed up! It meant everything to me that they were there.

The *pièce de résistance*, however, was that Al too was there! We had arranged for a laptop to show the videotape I had taken that Manning edited. So Al, in his beautiful voice, told his family, his grandchildren in particular, that he was not afraid to die, that he'd lived a good life and basically he was ready.

I've been told it was the best funeral ever. Al would have approved.

When the family got to my home that night, after the restaurant dinner, we placed the white urn on the mantelpiece above the living room fireplace, where we all sat exhausted, glum, and silent. Dan then found one of Al's beloved Yankee baseball caps and hung it on top of the urn, a brilliant touch, instantly making us all feel better. That's what Al would have wanted and where it will sit until my ashes join his.

I'VE DESCRIBED THE EFFECT SMELLS and sounds have on me—so much so that, fifty years ago, when I was pregnant with Carla and had just quit smoking my mentholated Salems, I kept a bottle of Vick's Vaporub to sniff for a fix; but our kids thought it was funny for me to sniff car exhausts. (Something to do with the carbon monoxide?) I'd go out of my way to stop at gas stations or stand near an idling car with its motor running.

But I have had another, unexpected, olfactory bonus: Some of our children and grandchildren emanate a particular scent that, if I close my eyes, makes me think Al could be there. Nancy runs away from me because I keep sniffing at her neck and hair, trying to conjure him up! He's still here in our family that way, which comforts me dearly, and if there is anything I've learned in life, it is the importance of family. During the years of my ordeal, each of our five children (they were also suffering the loss of their father) stepped up to the plate to be there for me. I call them my team. I have no doubt I could not have done as well as I did without their support. Nancy and Fred have been an immeasurable help with household problems, and Dan with financial advice. My grandchildren also have been beyond supportive—arranging dates with me, texting, calling, hiking, doing art projects with me, cooking dinners. Extraordinary human beings, Al used to kid people when they'd brag about their kids, "Hey, if you knew ours, seriously, you'd throw yours away!"

Between my family and my friends, the end of the tunnel may be growing light!

FACING MORTALITY HELPS DEFINE how you live your life. Try looking back at yours without adding violet or dark lenses. T'aint easy. I see my marriage as the best thing that ever happened to me, but it wasn't a Hollywood movie in Technicolor. I hope to convey to my children the lessons I've learned yet, at the same time, don't want to convey an idealized, unattainable model of perfection. At times, as I've pointed out, we were testy, bickering, jockeying for position, spiteful. But that's reality and only a miniscule part of the script of our lives, where work and determination overcame all.

When we are young we get periodic report cards, awards, medals, raises at work, and so on, assessing and appraising our efforts and abilities. But we don't get graded as adults.

If I were to assess me today, I'd give me a gold star for blending our two families together and giving Al the best ending available. I take comfort thinking I could assure that four-year-old Sondra, who held onto that tin mirror, that I turned out to be a good girl after all. Maybe not a famous scientist or movie star, but I believe that, when I'm gone, at least through my family, I contributed something in leaving this world a better place. And that's good enough.

In recent conversations, Carla has chastised me for not giving myself credit for overcoming the herculean task of breaking the cycle I inherited—that I turned my life around from the needy, self-destructive person I had been to a person she, at least, admires, making a happy life and being "an incredible lifesaver" with her Dad, as she perceived it. I know that my transformation didn't occur without Al, but I was also fiercely motivated to raise children nothing like the person I had been and instilling values nothing like the ones I had been taught.

As of this writing, I'm eighty-three, well into what I call Act 3. When I speak that number out loud, it sounds like somebody else's age! An octogenarian, *moi? C'est impossible.* I feel fortunate that I'm in excellent health and look much younger than my age. Maybe it's long telomeres, enzyme structures in cell chromosomes that control our biological clocks. When I was almost seventy I was chosen out of thousands of women to appear on an Oprah television program entitled *Age- Defying Women*, a big hoot. I take no medicine at all except for the smallest dosages of Lexapro and Trazadone I began during Al's illness, but I'm weaning off them. My dentist tells me I'll die with all my teeth; I still have a strong libido and the strength to do 150 daily not-so-good continuous pushups. My gynecologist has also said something positive about me health-wise, and my internist, upon examining me and my blood work, commented that one day he'd like to be as lucky as I am and would like to bottle me. It's entirely possible I'll finish this paragraph and drop dead, but as of this moment, knock on wood!

I remember that, for our television show *Second-Hand Strategies*, I interviewed the author Bel Kaufman, known for her best seller *Up the Down Staircase*; she exclaimed, "At my age, if I wake up in the morning and nothing hurts, I'm dead." Thankfully, nothing particularly hurts me—yet.

Clearly, if there is one thing I do not want to be, it is dead. Bearing that in mind, I don't consider it a contradiction in terms to say that, having learned a lesson from Al, I am not *afraid* to be dead. It's the getting there I don't relish. Still, I find that nature lets us down gently. Our faculties go as we age—eyesight, hearing, libido, blah, blah. By the time we've lived a long, full life (if we do), maybe we're not so unhappy about letting go. But I figure being dead is like it was before being conceived. Nothing. Absence. Void.

I suppose it would be nice to have religion with its comforting belief in a Heaven Hereafter, but I can't pretend what I don't believe. And having lived so many years so fully, I can truly accept knowing I'm coming near to its conclusion. Having spent most of my life with someone, the aloneness makes me feel incomplete at times. But if I'm not in denial, I guess I'm an optimist because, for the most part I feel hopeful, even pretty good.

Besides exercising, I eat as healthfully as I can, *trying* to keep my wine intake at one or so glasses, but I'll never give that up entirely. (As the *Rubaiyat of Omar Khayyam* puts it, "I often wonder what the vintner buys one-half so precious as the stuff he sells.") I've had work done on my face—a partial facelift thirty years ago, and now occasional injections when I feel inclined to look less like my grandmother. I could recite the many vicissitudes of aging, along with the petty negatives that plague—for example, having had to undergo two hip replacements down to my ugly bunions and the tummy fat I can't get rid of— but that's ego crap. I'm working very diligently on the pervasive problem of ego that, in my opinion, I (and most people) suffer from. It's clear to me how profoundly it gets in the way!

I'm glad to say my fragile self-confidence and need for constant approval no longer consume me. I've had the courage to rid myself of some toxic relationships as well. To quote an old Polish proverb: "When you feel pulled into other people's nonsense, repeat these words: *Not my circus, not my monkeys.*"

Being aware that my horizon is shorter, a few years ago I had a real glimpse into a future when I may become dependent on others, which wasn't a pretty picture. That taste came courtesy of my hip operation, when I was entirely dependent on my daughters, who came to wash my hair for me. However, if one day I'm permanently faced with helplessness, hopefully I'll manage it, too.

When I was young, life contained certain privileges that are no longer available. The trade-off is that I've accrued some wisdom along the way, and I certainly have clarity about who I am now. But negatives are inevitable. For me—to return to my metaphor of the blanket—it is like someone taking a nice warm blanket off and exposing me to the frigidity of marginalization or of being trivialized by, for example, typical geezer jokes. ("Ain't she spry"; "Ain't he agile for an old codger!"). But that comes with the territory.

AT THIS WRITING IT'S BEEN ALMOST TWO YEARS since Al died and around seven years since I became, for all intents and purposes, a widow. Life after Mrs.-hood finds me having conversations with him. Daily I stop in the room where his urn with the Yankee hat is sitting to discuss things. His pictures are everywhere in the house, and often I'll say to one of them, "Hi, darling," throwing a kiss, and it makes me feel better. I have his picture next to my car's steering wheel. Though my Alfie, my Alfredo, is gone, my love for him isn't. My mantra now is from Dr. Seuss: "Don't cry for what you lost, smile for what you had."

Of course living without him is ever-grievous. One day I'll think I'm "over" the worst of it and then, as happened yesterday, I'll have occasion to go into the one closet where some of his clothes that I couldn't get rid of remain, and I'm toast; collapsing into them, trying to retrieve his essence. But I've learned that there are positive things about living alone. I have no one to answer to on decisions like when or what to eat, where or where not to go, what or what not to spend, and I have gained some pride in my ability to do these new things well. Before Al died, I was always leaning on him to do everything for me. Now I've learned to do them for myself, so I'm a good example of what it means to teach a man to fish, and he'll have fish for a lifetime.

I'm grateful Al and I had that talk about what one of us would do when and if the other left first, because I still feel vital and viable enough to crave the company of men. Having my dear girlfriends and family fills some lonely hours, but I seek masculine friendship as well. However, I am not plugged into the thought of one as a lover. I have no skin in that game anymore! I was with one man only, for over fifty-five years, and the girl I was before him, that wanton creature, is no longer wantin'! Still, the loss of sexual intimacy is a big loss. Al can never be replaced, but that said, I recently read a *New York Times* article in which Jane Brody expounds upon sexual bereavement. "Disenfranchised grief" is a term she used that gives me pause. "You can honor your past," she writes, "treasure it, but you don't have to live in your past. People have an endless capacity to love."

And Sheryl Sandberg, in her book on grieving, *Option B*, writes: "Grief is the final act of love, and recovery from it is the necessary betrayal on which the future depends. There is only this one life, and we are the ones who are here to live it."

AMUSINGLY, A MAN ALL OF AGE FORTY-SIX has been persistent in trying to "see" me. When I incredulously asked him if he was hitting on me, a person old enough to be his grandmother, he said young women were complicated and he'd always had a thing for me! Although that's flattering, it's simply out of the question. There can never be another "us" for me, and certainly not with one younger than my son! As mentioned, I just need an arm, a companion to have dinner or see a movie with, and I'm glad to say I do have a few. Along this line, one of them, a dear, brilliant, funny guy in his mid-eighties, actually proposed marriage to me. Couldn't have surprised me more. He understands now that I will never remarry, that I deeply value his friendship but not his forever. I'm realistic enough to settle for an arm. Truth be told, I really want a heart or soul too, but Al was that and the best of that, and nobody could possibly come close. Still, there's no "poor me" for me. Since I'm already blessed with these few men friends, "arms," walks, laughs, movies, dinners, and masculine company are abundant. And yet, as Archy said in Don Marquis' verse, "There's a dance in the old dame yet, Mehitabel!" (However, perhaps if George Clooney came a-knockin', I'd add another part of the anatomy!) Anyway, if I have to, I'll dance in my rocking chair, because I cleave to the adage, "The best way to meet death is to exhaust life."

Friends extol and applaud my adjustment to widowhood. I recognize the ring of truth in that. I've come through.

SINGING LIGHT

Giddyup

Bonnie Raitt sang,
We can't change the past, but we can leave it behind.

NOTES TO CHILDREN: First of all, life is messy. Own that. If I were the kind of old lady, a cheery, chubby, white-haired granny sitting on a rocking chair, shawl thrown over shoulders, knitting patiently, while the aroma of warm apple pie wafts from the oven, and I offered the following advice, you might be more receptive to it.

But I am a size six, tinted-haired Nonnie (my grandchildren's name for me) with a periodically injection-filled face usually splattered with tons of makeup, who does Pilates and yoga, the first one to make a fool of myself to get on a dance floor and the last to quit clothes shopping, or seeking a laugh. So here's my two cents anyway: The hard work is dealing with disappointment and adversity. No way of getting out of it, and nobody to do it for you.

And if I've acquired any clarity in my long life, it's this: Whatever hand you're dealt, don't fold your confidence too readily. There's always hope for a better card. And if and when you fall, get back up on that horse and hang on till your last breath.

In La Jolla, on top of Mt. Soledad, stands a veteran's memorial where you can find a plaque with Al in his army uniform.

In Washington, D.C., at the Smithsonian, you can find Al's costume from *Space Cadets*. I think of these as his "pyramids."

In my prologue, I questioned my reasons for writing this memoir (including a need to leave *my* pyramid: "Hey, Sondra was here!")

Perhaps the engine that drives me is some indomitable spirit or just downright stubbornness, but I do not intend to go gently into that good night. And I don't intend to stumble over something that's behind me. As I said, I've come to believe that all the pain I suffered in my early life, onerous as it was, has resulted in who I am today, and I like who I am today. I'm still a work in progress, but I am not defined by my past.

I continue to learn every day. One of my "arms," a neighbor and a terrific guy who is also a widower, has taught me the simplest and hardest of lessons. If I'm distressed about something, he'll say, "It's okay! Really, it's okay." At first I thought that a bit too simplistic, but in time I've learned, yeah—so you forgot your something or other, or lost your something or other, or made a mistake. . . . It's not the end of the world, it's okay, it's all good! Cut your octogenarian self some slack!

Another great neighbor (and "arm") recently wrote me a little letter prefaced with, "It didn't take long to realize that you are an extreme empath, filled with compassion and the ability to connect

SINGING LIGHT

with others." I like that. Had I been to the manor born, with a different and perfect life, I might not have been as empathetic or insightful as I've had to become.

As for letters, I came across one that Al wrote to me many years ago. So I'll finalize my list of reasons for this memoir by saying that, ultimately, maybe this is for him, and somewhere he knows I'm doing him proud by holding up—and with the family intact—that I've got this!

I'll let him have the last word, for at the end of that letter he wrote:

> Xmas 1998 — Merry, merry!
>
> My darling, (and you will always be "my darling" and the love of my life!)
>
> I wish you all the things you would wish for yourself. I feel lessened when I cannot always make you happy.
>
> You are still (without doubt) the most beautiful and wonderful woman, and I'm a lucky man.
>
> Don't ever doubt my love for you... it is strong and unconditional. We're going to go through a beautiful stage of our lives together, and yes, there will be some tough days. But from the first moment on the River Queen ours was a spectacular + special love. Perhaps in years to come someone will write about it.
>
> Thank you, for being you and for being with me. I cherish that.
>
> All my love,
> Alfredo

ACKNOWLEDGMENTS

This memoir was built on the support and enlightenment of my family and friends. Along with my husband Al, they were instrumental in making it a reality. I'm the lucky recipient of the unfailing assistance of my daughter, Carla Siegel, and my friends Ed Fitzpatrick and Al Schwartz, in addition to the helpful comments of my other children, Gary Fisher and Nina Laul. I'm grateful also to my editor, Barry Sheinkopf, who knew when to judge, nudge, and applaud.

I suppose now my life really is "an open book," though I trust some mystery remains, fodder, perhaps for my next memoir when I get older (we do get older, but not necessarily old!)—and, fingers crossed, along with my soul-sistahs Joy Anderson, Mimi Elfenbein, and Judy Sultan to inspire me, along with my children, their spouses, and my darling grandchildren who are a never ending source of delight.

www.ingramcontent.com/pod-product-compliance
Lightning Source LLC
LaVergne TN
LVHW041333080426
835512LV00006B/439